FRANCHISING FREEDOM!

15 Franchisors And Franchising Experts Share Best Thinking And Proven Strategies For Successfully Franchising A Business

W&M

Franchising Freedom!

First published in September 2020

W&M

ISBN 978-1-912774-70-8

Editors: Peter Daly-Dickson, Andrew Priestley

A CIP catalogue record for this book is available from the British Library.

Disclaimer: *Franchising Freedom!* is intended for information and education purposes only. This book does not constitute specific legal, financial, clinical or commercial advice unique to your situation.

The views and opinions expressed in this book are those of the authors and do not reflect those of the Publisher and Resellers, who accept no responsibility for loss, damage or injury to persons or their belongings as a direct or indirect result of reading this book.

All people mentioned in case studies have been used with permission, and/or have had names, genders, industries and personal details altered to protect client confidentiality. Any resemblance to persons living or dead is purely coincidental.

Contents

Passion And Empathy

Foreword - Stan Friedman

When Peter contacted me about this project, it sounded like an ambitious undertaking, on an impossible timeline. Well, far be it from me to ever question his ability again, when it comes to executing against vision. My name is Stan Friedman and for 30+ years, I have lived, loved and breathed franchising. I have done so as a franchisor, a founder, a supplier and thought leader and now, as a franchise podcaster, as well.

As this book will teach, franchise licenses are usually granted with rights to operate within certain geographical territories. That said, there are certain common threads in franchising that simply know no boundaries. No matter the market segment, concept, or brand, the continent, country or languages spoken locally, these common threads that I refer to are *passion* and *empathy*.

In franchising, these threads are ubiquitous. As a culture, franchising is always, people first, meaning that as a model for doing business, franchising is far more relational, than transactional. Therefore, at its core, any franchise brand, scaling for sustainable growth, will possess high levels of both, from the top down.

I am also happy to say that these same threads are stitched in abundance, throughout the pages of this book. The core competencies of the book's contributors are diverse, each sharing unique information, representing different aspects of the franchising lexicon, much like points on a compass. With passion and empathy, each author serves up another puzzle piece, that when fully assembled, enables you to better appreciate and deploy this fabulous business model. As you will quickly learn, when executed properly, the freedom that franchising provides, is both quantum and exponential.

I very proudly endorse Franchising Freedom as a "common sense" tool that will help you navigate your journey toward franchise ownership and further your learning, in terms of how to "own your business/own your life."

Stan Friedman

Principal Consultant - Sensible Franchising

Partner - FRM Solutions

Host and Executive Producer - Franchise Today Podcast

Affiliations: (IFA) International Franchise Association

Southeast Franchise Form

www.linkedin.com/in/4stanfriedman

www.sensiblefranchising.com

Franchising Matters

Preface - Peter Daly-Dickson

When you look under the hood, it can be surprising to find out that many of the businesses you know and interact with are franchises. And for good reason.

One of the most difficult things to achieve in a growing business is a consistent and reliable experience and journey for customers. It's why there's often a 'risk to refer' a business, as you can't guarantee your friend or colleague will receive the same experience that prompted your referral.

Franchising provides that guarantee.

And, provided the franchising business owner has the right support and advice, it's why successful franchises grow so rapidly.

And why franchisees, with the right mindset and tools, can achieve results in a timeframe that would leave most small businesses owners green with envy.

Franchising Freedom is unique in that it speaks to business owners looking to grow through franchising, existing franchisors and franchisees. The more that each knows about each other, the better for all concerned.

You've done the hard work of getting to where you are.

Now, tap into the hard-won advice, insights and strategies of the 14 successful franchisors and international franchising experts we've brought together in this book, to supercharge your own journey to franchising freedom.

As they say in France, 'bon courage'!

Peter Daly-Dickson

Founder & CEO, Macanta

www.macantacrm.com/freedom

LinkedIn: www.macantacrm.com/peterli

Franchising Success – The Right Way to Get 'Franchise-Ready'

Shireen Smith

If you want to take your business to the next level, franchising provides a less capital-intensive way to grow nationally and internationally.

The franchisee promotes your brand by following your successful proven path, while you provide support with marketing, access to trusted suppliers, systems, and other resources. Training becomes a core part of your business activity because you are helping your franchisees to build a business that replicates yours.

If you have a successful business which you want to expand consider whether:

- franchising is the right step for *you* personally?
- you have the right skills and resources.
- your business is at *the right stage* for franchising.
- the business is suited to franchising.

An important issue is whether your brand is distinctive and legally protectable. This is discussed in my forthcoming book: *Brand Tuned - How to Create a Distinctive, Inimitable Brand That Wins Business in a Noisy World?*

Although the points mentioned above are all important, here I focus on the fundamental question whether your brand is legally effective.

One role of a brand is to function as a barrier to entry against competitors. This is not necessarily the yardstick by which designers create a visual identity. Therefore, before considering franchising, or a business exit, assess how distinctive your branding is legally, and what issues you might face when protecting its intellectual property (IP).

Your brand name and designs determine how memorable you are and impact your ability to attract sales. If the brand doesn't work as IP, it will be incapable of uniquely identifying your business long term. You will encounter problems protecting it, especially in key markets overseas.

Unless the brand is legally aligned to your business strategy, it could result in wasted time and cost down the line. For example, Zumba needed a highly distinctive name to sell its wide variety of goods and services internationally. A weaker, descriptive name would not have enabled it to roll out the business as it has done. The company would have hit problems securing registrations in different countries. It would have needed different branding in some countries, and its overseas trademarking experience would have been messy and costly.

What Is IP?

IP is an umbrella term that refers to five legal disciplines which impact creations of the mind:

- patents
- trademarks
- copyrights,
- designs, and
- confidential information.

The creations covered include:

- inventions
- designs
- written materials
- images
- music
- secret recipes
- brand names
- software
- and more.

Each IP law governs different subject matter, and sometimes several laws impact a creation. For example, copyright, designs and trademarks are all relevant to logos.

IP such as know-how, and trade secrets relies on confidentiality laws for protection.

Know-how, such as the accumulated skills and experience that resides in your business should be turned into an asset of your company by properly capturing it in your systems and processes. Once preserved this know-how will be held in your business, and is at less risk of being forgotten, or lost, such as when an employee leaves your employ.

Systemising and updating your processes to preserve your company's know-how also happens to be what is necessary to have a well-functioning business that can run without you. This systemisation work is critical in enabling you to run a better business. Doing so frees up your time and resources. It also enables you to prepare the all-important 'operations manual' you need to franchise your business.

Why Is IP Important For *Your* Brand?

Franchising requires a big capital outlay. People often take out a sizeable loan to set up a franchise. In practice, they don't dedicate a budget to fundamentals such as assessing their IP and securing necessary protections.

People sometimes jump into franchising hastily both feet first, disregarding fundamentals such as addressing their IP. They don't review their brand assets for distinctiveness from a legal perspective, and risk incurring far greater costs undoing ill-considered actions.

A do-it-yourself (DIY) trademark registration is not the right foundation on which to build a franchise operation, even if you only franchise in the UK. Litigation can and does arise, and the brand is vulnerable if its trademark specification is inadequate. Many DIY registrations are bare bones, miss essential classes and are poorly drafted. They do not adequately protect the business.

Nor is it widely appreciated, even by business lawyers that a trademark registration in the UK and EU does not protect you against trademark infringement claims. For example, Microsoft had an EU trademark registration for SkyDrive but was sued by Sky. The court decided it was infringing on Sky's brand so that Microsoft had to rebrand to OneDrive.

Your entire business foundation rests on legally owning your brand name and assets.

One business I know had to rebrand shortly after embarking on a franchise operation. Rebranding is never easy or affordable but is made doubly costly if you have already embarked on franchising and prepared your franchise brochures and other collateral.

A recent report by CompuMark, a Thomson Reuters company in PR Newswire: Trademark Infringement Rising Year On Year revealed that 85% of brands experienced trademark infringement in 2019, showing a steady upward trend from 81% in 2018 and 74% in 2017.

Intangible assets are more important than ever to business, yet many entrepreneurs are unaware of the significance of IP. Leaving IP until after a brand is created risks building it on a foundation of sand.

Failing to review your IP runs the risk of costly litigation spanning many years. This would jeopardise the sale of the business or reduce its price and would adversely affect your franchising journey too.

So, focus on improving your business before taking any steps towards franchising.

Franchising And Licensing

Licensing your business format and IP, is essentially what franchising involves.

Licensing is just the legal name for what's involved to franchise a business. Indeed, licensing is involved in many other well-known ways of monetising IP such as brand licensing, character merchandising, and know how licensing.

The difference between franchising and licensing a business format is simply that franchising is an established way of licensing a business format.

Franchising has its own rules and bodies that oversee the activity. However, it is perfectly possible legally to achieve the same end as franchising by using a less formal arrangement to license your business format. However, the laws of some countries, such as the USA, disallow licensing of business formats.

In the USA franchising is heavily regulated and fines are imposed on any business that avoids the regulations by licensing its business format outside a franchising arrangement.

Franchising is the only way to license your business format in the USA and other countries that disallow a less formal approach of licensing your business format. In such countries you cannot escape the regulations: if you are effectively franchising your business by using a simple licensing arrangement. The regulations will deem you to be franchising. On the Azrights blog I've written about this: *Licensing and Franchising -What is the Difference and Does it Matter?*

Licensing your business format instead of franchising it is an option for businesses located in the UK as the UK franchising regulations do not disallow informal arrangements.You could therefore test the suitability of franchising by licensing your business format initially instead of franchising it.

There are advantages in licensing your business format as an interim solution before opting for franchising because there are few formalities involved.

The upfront costs being lower mean you can focus your budget initially on building a sturdier business, putting your IP in order, and then reap many of the potential gains that franchising offers by licensing your business format to interested third parties.

Laying The Groundwork For Licensing

By having your branding reviewed, and protecting your IP appropriately, you will be better equipped to fend off problems that successful brands invariably attract.

Licensing is relatively simple once you've sorted out your IP and transferred it to a holding company. That company grants licences to use its IP to any licensees you appoint.

Putting your IP in a holding company is a worthwhile action to take anyway to shield your valuable IP assets and ring fence them, in the event of litigation or insolvency.

With this groundwork in place you can appoint a licensee

using an arrangement loosely based around franchising that is less prescriptive. You can decide how to grant permission to third parties to use your business format taking as much control as you want.

Licensing Agreement

The licensing agreement will impose many of the same controls as a typical franchising deal, such as requiring your licensee to comply with your established ways of running the business as stipulated in your operations manuals. If you want, you can disallow the slightest difference in the business format in case it damages your brand. You can include quality control provisions, and sanctions against a licensee who attempts to break out and introduce their own ideas.

The arrangement leaves you in control of the brand, and on how the licensee runs the business.

A benefit of trying out licensing is that you can start with a licensee you know and trust and use a more flexible route fashioned to suit your requirements. You will learn what is involved to train licensees in the way you operate your business.

Giving someone else access to your proven systems, processes and IP means you get to test the waters in real life, identify issues that need to be addressed with your first licensees and iron out kinks before embarking on franchising and the larger associated costs involved.

Having tested the arrangement nationally using this simpler, cheaper approach to achieve similar ends means you prepare for franchising in a way that both improves your business anyway and gets your business ready for franchising, and increases your revenues.

If you aspire to have an international franchise, it is doubly important to review your IP and give yourself time to put your brand on a firm footing. To enter markets worldwide needs an international trademark strategy.

Whether you decide to franchise or to grow organically, I hope this chapter will have raised your awareness of the importance of having your IP and brand professionally assessed and protected.

About Shireen Smith

Shireen Smith is an intellectual property lawyer and business advisor specialising in trademarks, brands and licensing. Her interest in business led her to in-house positions at Coopers & Lybrand and then Reuters. She returned briefly to private practice at the international law firm Eversheds while raising her children, before founding Azrights, a law firm 15 years ago.

Shireen is a trained journalist and writes extensively about brands, business and IP. She is the host of the podcast Brand Tuned, which provides ideas and inspiration to develop the brand and business

She has published articles in numerous journals, and been a regular speaker at the British Library, the London School of Economics and at conferences for the legal industry and entrepreneurs. She is the author of two books, Legally Branded and Intellectual Property Revolution, which focus on the impact of the internet on business calling for a new approach to IP in the 21st century.

Contact Shireen Smith

https://azrights.com/

https://www.linkedin.com/in/shireensmith/

https://twitter.com/ShireenSmith

https://www.youtube.com/shireensmithAzrights

https://www.instagram.com/shireensmith/

https://www.facebook.com/shireensmithbrands

https://azrights.com/podcast/

Inside The Mind Of The Prospective Franchisee: How Franchisors Can Show They're One Of The 'Good Ones'

Marisa Rauchway

As a franchise attorney, on any given day, I receive a call from a prospective franchisee looking to purchase their very first franchise. I can usually tell within the first five minutes that the person on the phone is new to franchising, as typically a mix of both excitement and anxiety permeates their voice.

A typical conversation often goes as follows – the individual explains that they have never owned their own business before, but has found what seems to be a great opportunity to start something of their own ... with a little help. Maybe they are currently in a corporate job that doesn't fulfill them, and they are looking to try something entirely new. Or maybe they recently lost their job, and see this as a way to restart their career going down a different path. They have often spoken with the Franchisor and love the concept, and may or may not have attended a Discovery Day or spoken with other franchisees in the system. They have often received a thick Franchise Disclosure Document, and may have flipped through it, or (tried to) read every word, or – more often than not – have been using it as a coaster while trying to find someone to explain the daunting document to them.

Regardless, the conversation almost always turns to their concerns, and what keeps them up at night while they decide if this is something they really want to do.

These concerns - deeply heartfelt and very real – are varied, though typically revolve around one central theme: *what if I do my best, but I can't make this work? Then what? Can I get out? Is my retirement nest egg at risk? Will I be able to provide for my family?*

These concerns also involve other common restrictions placed on franchisees – *can I keep my current job if I buy this franchise? Are there any restrictions on where my family members can work?*

And for those who have read through the franchise agreement - *why does this contract just seem so favorable to the Franchisor? Is anything in here negotiable? Is all of this really fair?*

As a Franchisor, the answers to these questions may seem straightforward and simple.

There must be certain restrictions in place to protect the system, and, by extension, each individual franchisee. And while you may have a different response to a prospective franchisee's concerns than another franchisor, you are certainly not looking to take advantage of anyone, and you want your franchisees to be wildly successful. For prospective franchisees that seem like a great fit for your concept, you want to be able to show them you're one of the *good ones* – a franchisor who they can trust as a partner for years to come.

In one sense, franchise attorneys and other professionals can certainly help here. We can explain how franchising works in general, and what is (and is not) normal with franchisors across the board, and critically why certain provisions are often found in franchise agreements.

That being said, this general information can only go so far. In my years of working with prospective franchisees and franchisors, I have noticed certain key similarities with Franchisors who are able to satisfy prospective franchisees that they are a good fit in which to invest their time and money, and those that drive these prospects away. Here are my takeaways:

1. Truly Honor A Prospective Franchisee's Concerns

In my view, it is critically important to really show a potential franchisee that you understand why they have the concerns they do. This is true whether your system has taken the position that you will not, as a matter of policy, change a single word in your franchise agreements, or whether your system is open to negotiating a limited number of provisions in your agreement.

I have all too often seen a Franchisor dismiss – or worse yet – criticize a potential franchisee's concern or request for a change to a franchise agreement as *unreasonable*, leaving the franchisee with the feeling that the Franchisor will not take the time to appreciate a Franchisee's concerns moving forward.

On the other hand, I have seen a wonderful tone set at the start of a relationship between a Franchisor and Franchisee, even where a Franchisor is unable to accommodate a franchisee's request to make a change to a franchise agreement, by the Franchisor merely demonstrating a true understanding of the Franchisee's concern and what else the system offers the Franchisee that may (or may not) assuage that concern.

The bottom line is this – you do not have to upend your entire franchise system for a prospective franchisee who has concerns about your system. Often times, opening the line of communications to address their concerns in a respectful, honest manner, can show a prospective franchisee that you, the franchisor, may still be a good fit for them moving forward.

2. Make Sure Whoever Is Speaking To (Or Negotiating) A Franchise Agreement Reflects Your Company's Values.

Recently, I had a client call me very excited about becoming one of the first franchisees for a new fast-casual concept. She conveyed to me that she had spoken at length with the Franchisor and the Franchisor had – in keeping with the first point above –truly understood some of her initial concerns and had really put her mind at ease about being a franchisee in the system. She and I then had a conversation about the proposed franchise agreement, and some very limited changes we agreed were reasonable to propose.

After presenting these limited changes, we received a response from a representative of the Franchisor – not the owner who my client had spoken with directly – that was a wholesale rejection of such changes, as well as a criticism of even asking for such changes as *unreasonable*. This entirely soured my client's interest in the franchise. Ultimately, the owner of the franchise and my client were able to speak once again directly, and, after some additional back-and-forth, many of her requested changes were ultimately accepted. Upon speaking once again with the Franchisor's representative, he said he was simply responding in what he thought was in the best interest of the Franchisor.

It is critically important that the individuals engaging with your potential franchisees – whether outside counsel or in-house representatives – understand the tone you want to set with your prospective franchisees. While they undoubtedly have the best interest of the brand in mind, keep in mind that *soft skills* matter. Although you often will not be able to give a potential franchisee everything they request, it is the way you handle these requests that often set the tone for your entire relationship. In fact, I have also seen negotiations where a franchisee gets *everything* they want, but the way in which the Franchisor's representative treated the franchisee in the process entirely kills the deal any way.

3. Give Specific Examples Of What You Have Done In The Past To Assist Franchisees, Particularly In Times Of Trouble

The COVID-19 outbreak has certainly disrupted much of the franchise industry, and has undoubtedly made certain prospective franchisees wary of becoming a franchisee. That said, troubling times provide an incredible opportunity for a franchisor to show a potential franchisee that the Franchisor truly understands the worries of its franchisees and is invested in their success. For example, Franchisors who agreed to modifications of their system requirements during government lockdowns so that Franchisees could survive (and even thrive) in these unprecedented times – and who regularly communicated with their franchisees about all of the franchisor's efforts to support franchisees during this time -- have a wonderful story to tell prospective franchisees. Not only does this show what a Franchisor is willing to do when franchisees are struggling during a pandemic, but it also potentially shows a new franchisee what the Franchisor is willing to do in general to help a system flourish.

In sum, it is often said that entering into a franchisor-franchisee relationship is similar to getting married – each party wants to be sure they are comfortable with one another for a long term commitment. It is therefore imperative for Franchisors to understand that it is often not simply what is in black and white in their franchise agreements that matters. Although the language of the agreements are certainly critically important, the way in which a Franchisor treats a potential franchisee and a potential franchisee's concerns can not only set the tone for the relationship moving forward, but also whether a relationship ends up existing at all.

The above article provides general information, and is not intended as legal advice and does not create an attorney-client relationship of any kind.

About Marisa Rauchway

Marisa Rauchway is the owner and founder of Rauchway Law, a Franchise and Business law practice with offices in New Jersey and New York. Marisa has years of experience assisting clients navigate legal issues both in and out of court, including countless prospective franchisees, emerging concept franchisors, current single and multi-unit franchise operators, and businesses across a wide range of industries. Marisa was named as a 2019 *New Leader of the Bar* by the New Jersey Law Journal and was selected for inclusion in the 2017 and 2018 editions of the New Jersey Super Lawyers – Rising Stars for Business Litigation. Marisa is a graduate of Princeton University, Boston University Law School, and earned a Franchise Management Certificate in 2016 from Georgetown University.

Contact Marisa Rauchway

www.rauchwaylaw.com

https://www.linkedin.com/in/marisa-rauchway-sverdlov-36b75022

https://www.facebook.com/rauchwaylaw

https://open.spotify.com/show/62XJwC9cgPkThbhaelkMGU

The Big Game of Franchising

Stephen Maeker

I grew up in Flatonia, Texas, where my graduating class had 32 people. I'm a little guy, but athletic. I quarterbacked the Flatonia Bulldogs my senior year, going to the state semi-finals. I went to the State UIL tennis tournament both my junior and senior year and finished third in State.

Growing up in a small town was a great experience. You learned how to get along with one another and to truly value a diverse community.

I married my soul mate Christy in 2006. She is the Director of Counseling for Katy ISD, which – unlike my hometown – serves 84,000+ students. She and I both also serve as elders at our church in Katy. We have two children, Barnes, an entrepreneur, is pursuing his dream of becoming a music performer and producer. Our daughter Sydney is a highly accomplished cellist.

Hook 'em Horns! It is fair to say that The University of Texas runs deep in my family and I am a third generation Longhorn. My paternal Granddaddy was Phi Beta Kappa as an undergrad, when his law school career cut short when he joined the

US Navy to serve in WW II. Mom earned her Master's in Nutrition Science. Dr. Lorene Rogers – a past president of UT - served as her mentor and became a friend. When I was 12, Dr. Rogers gave me one of my most prized possessions: a 1977 Longhorns football poster signed by the team, with Coach Fred Akers' and football legend Earl Campbell's signatures right in the middle. This now hangs over my desk and serves as an inspiration. I earned my BBA in Management and Finance from UT and completed my MBA in Entrepreneurial Ventures there, though my Master's was conferred by The University of Southern California. Our daughter Sydney will be a fourth generation Longhorn, transferring to UT from Cleveland Institute of Music beginning Fall 2020 to complete her undergrad and pursue either law or medicine.

Four men shaped my career, which has been largely in franchising.

Granddaddy, a rural mail carrier for 40 years in Waelder, Texas, built wealth by buying stock on margin. He initially bought a leading tobacco stock in the 1960s, betting lawyers would never prove cigarettes caused cancer. Things just took off from there. Papa, my father's dad, raised Charolais cattle and sold cotton seed. In 2007, our family received a 100-year Texas heritage award from then-Governor Rick Perry. Dad, an Accountant/Banker, worked for two companies his entire career. He taught me what giving your word to someone meant. He is an Army veteran who served during the Berlin crisis. My beloved mentor, Joe Culver at UT, opened the franchising door for me in 1988 when he introduced me to Dave Pearce, HR manager for Mr. Gatti's Pizza.

Dave gave me a one semester HR internship where I

summarized drug screen results and DWI records for potential delivery drivers. The experience went well and one day I found myself in an executive team meeting where the founder, L.D. Brinkman, was frustrated with store performance and profitability. I pitched Mystery Shopping as a possible solution and the next thing I knew I was a college kid with a grandmotherly secretary helping me develop and implement a local program that quickly went national. Many of my friends served as Shoppers as we were all broke college students always looking for their next meal. The stores in Austin consistently executed the Operations manual so the dining experience/scores were consistently good. The farther away the stores got from corporate, the worse the financial performance was. Enter a revamped training program with a focus on operational consistency.

The *first down* of my professional career came when I left Mr. Gatti's upon graduating from The University of Texas in 1990 to work for Mobil Oil. I had seven job offers and signed with Mobil because they paid me $10 more a year than Coca-Cola. I held numerous positions with Mobil, but my favorite was being a Franchise Consultant to 35 franchisees in Los Angeles. I had South Central when the Rodney King riots happened and watched as our gas pumps were ripped out of the ground and wheeled down the street on a dolly.

Late one night when I was doing my monthly night ride, I noticed a mysterious truck on site at a station in East LA. Watching from across the street, I realized the franchisee was buying cheaper/lower quality fuel on the black market. I politely tapped the driver on his shoulder, took a picture of him dispensing the fuel in the tanks, and asked for the invoice, which he gave. The next day I went back to his station with my boss, pulled out the franchise agreement, and terminated him on the spot. He had paid zero attention to the contractual language of the franchise agreement. This was a major fumble continues to inform my work today.

After six years predominantly on the West Coast with Mobil, I was sacked by homesickness and moved back to Texas where my Little League baseball coach's wife was a Board member for the Lower Colorado River Authority (LCRA), which I refer to as a quasi-franchise.

My role with LCRA was to contractually secure the electric load of 26 of their 44 wholesale customers, all municipalities. My ticket into the City Councils became performing a Cost of Service study which helped them understand their rate classes to their municipal customers. Electric rates helped fund the General Fund, which is how cities are run. If three of the five City Council members owned businesses, it seemed that the lion's share was borne by homeowners. If none of the Council members were business owners, vice versa. My goal was to add value and support to my customers, which is exactly what a good franchisor does.

I gained a lot of yardage when I joined TGI Friday's, then the world's largest casual dining restaurant chain. I oversaw strategic planning and financial reporting for 150 restaurants in 50 countries and two strategic joint ventures, Asia and Latin America.

My International COO boss, Richard Snead, who later became CEO, was frustrated with my predecessor, a highly intelligent Harvard MBA, as he felt he did not understand the business. While I was nowhere in Harvard's league intelligence-wise, I was smart enough to figure out that everyone understands color: when green means go, yellow means proceed with caution and red means stop.

Enter the creation of the Balanced Scorecard which is what I used to educate the leadership team to help run the international business. Outside of G&A, one of our largest expenses was fighting piracy, where a restaurateur would open up a Friday's, copy the menu, décor, etc., but forget to do one minor thing: actually become a franchisee!

I enjoyed the restaurant business, so calling an audible to Jack-in-the-Box as an Area Manager seemed to make sense. The JBX Executive Team was amazing. They entrusted me with me into taking on the worst performing 20 company-operated store area in the entire organization. It nearly killed me but within three years, things were turned around and on-track. JBX was focused on converting company stores to franchises and I participated in strategy to convert. Ensuring unannounced food safety and operational standard audits on a quarterly basis with both company and franchised restaurants was critical.

I benched franchising for the next five years, becoming the National Director of Employer Relations & Career Services for Alta Colleges where I oversaw graduate placement in field of study for 20 campuses. This was an opportunity to develop talented teams and I loved every minute of it.

Five years into Alta, an Executive Recruiter contacted me, this time on behalf of Vancouver, Washington-based Papa Murphy's Take N Bake Pizza. John Barr, an ex-oil man from Pennzoil, drafted me as the Vice President of Franchise Sales. Pretty quick we had a substantial deal on the table with a family from Dubai. The fun of logistics and product sourcing became reality. Towards the end of my stint with PMI, I met industry leader FranChoice and wanted them to provide qualified candidates. The PMI Board ultimately disagreed and we politely parted ways.

This allowed me to run a quarterback sneak and for the last 8½ years, I have been a nationally published Franchise Consultant with FranChoice, the national champion franchise consulting team. I've championed numerous candidates across the country into realizing their entrepreneurial dreams. I represent 150 prescreened concepts, both retail and service. I am a free matchmaker, using a process similar to the way I met my wife Christy, via E-Harmony. It's about matching what the candidate deems important as key characteristics with franchisors that possess the same traits. Minimum net worth and liquidity, territory availability, transferrable skill set, buying an existing business vs starting one from scratch (98% of my deals are new start-ups) all factor in. Pre-Covid, the normal investigation time ran about two months.

One franchisor I represent is industry leading powerhouse, Sola Salon Studios. Christy and I are proud, award-winning, multi-unit franchisees. We developed our first Sola in College Station and now are about to open Bryan, Texas, and are proud to have positively coached over 50 beauty professionals' lives. Unlike in a traditional salon, all our team of salon professionals does is serve their clients in their private, one-on-one secured suites personalized to their individual tastes. They play their own music, sell their own retail and work whenever they want to. We adore the brand and our family of beauty professionals.

What is the playbook of franchising?

It's buying into a proven model to follow a gameplan for *potential* success. Candidates – sometimes like rookie players – typically come to me with five primary motivations: downsizing, diversification, change, immigration visa or wanting to leave a legacy.

Advantages of franchising can include proven systems, partnership and peer groups, tax ramifications, national brand recognition/buying power, real estate acquisition and marketing expertise.

However, the franchising game is not for everyone. Franchisees must follow the rules because if not – as with the Mobil Oil franchise scenario – they go out of bounds with the franchise agreement and may be terminated. Each domestic franchisor must annually produce a Franchise Disclosure Document (FDD) which contains 23 items. An FDD is a playbook, written in consistent/uniform language, protective of the franchisor. Minimum net worth and liquidity targets are set. Not all franchisors are created equally.

A franchisor cannot ever guarantee financial performance.

The FranChoice game plan involves sequential plays that starts with an introductory call. A brief Confidential Questionnaire is then sent, after which a phone/Internet-based consultation is scheduled. Next, the candidate's model is written, which leads me to identify a short list of franchisors to whom I send territory checks.

When concept introductions are done and I've formally introduced the candidate to the targeted franchisor, I use another football field analogy explaining the investigation sequence process. It starts with a concept introduction call with the franchisor – at the goal line. FDD dissemination/review, unit economics, marketing, operations, real estate/site acquisition – all within the first 50 yards.

The candidate should now start to visualize themselves in the end zone. The candidate then enters validation where they hear from existing franchisees on the team. During this time, they are working on funding, determining if a corporation should be formed, and working to ensure they understand the contractual language of the franchise agreement.

Once this has all been done, they attend a Discovery Day (now typically via Zoom/webinar technology due to Covid), which involves meeting the leadership team and helping to assess mutual fit, where a go or no-go decision is made by both sides. If the decision is to jointly move forward, franchise agreements are prepared and sent out (typically via DocuSign), the candidate holds them for seven days after which they can execute and fund their franchise agreement.

Lastly, the franchisor countersigns the franchise agreement, and that's when the fun really begins ... TOUCHDOWN!

About Stephen Maeker

Stephen Maeker is a nationally published Franchise Consultant with industry leader FranChoice. Prior to joining FranChoice in 2012, he spent the bulk of his career in high-level franchising positions with four industry leading brands. He lives in Houston, Texas, with his wife, Christy, and French bulldog, Harold.

Contact Stephen Maeker

Email *smaeker@FranChoice.com*

Website *www.FranChoice.com/smaeker*

LinkedIn *https://www.linkedin.com/in/stephen-maeker-8b92872*

Facebook *https://www.facebook.com/stephen.maeker*

Without A Net: Pitfalls to Avoid Vs Successful Franchise Strategies

Matt Frentheway

As a child back in the 1970s, I once asked my parents what a green light meant at intersections. They told me that the green light (of course!) means "Go!" Inevitably, as parents are wont to do, the next time they approached an intersection, they turned to me and asked what the green light meant. I replied, "Go Man Go!" I have been living this "Go Man Go!" lifestyle ever since.

Later in life I realized I wanted to help others also get to where they want to go.

Being an eyewitness to the tragedy of the 9/11 attacks in 2001 was a huge wakeup call and turning point for me, not unlike many Americans and people from all around the world.

Shortly before that fateful day I had found personal satisfaction and business success assisting many people in achieving their financial goals as a Financial Advisor with renowned global financial institution UBS PaineWebber. This experience was invaluable in helping me formulate one of the most critical business strategies one should employ in every business endeavor--matchmaking your goals to the right financial investment and not the other way around. I'll get into those details in a moment, but after starting a couple of independent businesses, in 2015 I decided to stretch my boundary and embark on a new entrepreneurial path, personally building a business that I could turn into a franchise and subsequently helping others realize their dream of franchise ownership.

These dual trajectories led me to the most satisfying professional journey of my life and lit my passion for providing invaluable tools for others who seek the freedom of owning their own business through franchise ownership. I'm thrilled to share a few of the most critical lessons I have learned through trial and error and through the (sometimes) painful leap into unchartered waters, most often without a net.

Match Your Franchise To Your Personality

With over 4,000 franchise opportunities available to investors seeking the freedom that owning a business can provide, the process out of the gate can seem overwhelming and stressful.

There is so much to consider, including location to type of businesses to consider. From restaurants and cafes to salon/spas, retail, physical fitness and education or healthcare, where do you start? One of the things I have always advised my clients is, *the best way to eat an elephant is one bite at a time.*

Here are some strategies that can help make the process less daunting:

- **Take your journey one step at a time** and more importantly, don't try to fit a square peg into a round hole when considering a new business venture. Too many franchise investors make the mistake of trying to fit their personality into a franchise opportunity that, at the end of the day, is not a good match. For example, if you're not a night owl, don't even think about opening a restaurant just because you love their menu or their brand. Because inevitably, despite your best efforts to hire the best staff on the planet, your time will be needed at your franchise and you'll end up resenting the late nights you may need to keep on occasion.
- **Begin first with the focus on your own personality traits** and how those might fit into a franchise that synergizes with those characteristics and goals for what you want your life to look and feel like. This critical step is the first thing I advise and flush out with all my candidates. I spend a considerable amount of time helping potential business owners identify their personality

traits that will perfectly align with a franchise that fits these characteristics and not the other way around.

- **Embrace the Steven Covey method of** ***begin with the end in mind.*** Determine your own needs in terms of freedom, flexibility and income goals along with how to balance your work life with the needs of your personal life, your family, your financial future and your sense of wellbeing. Consider your personality traits across the board--are you an introvert or extrovert; are you a detail-oriented person or a big-picture thinker? Are you task oriented or a manager? Are you a self-starter or a team player? Do you value freedom in your life over workaholism? Does your lifestyle and passion veer toward customer service, recreation, fine dining, healthy living or *retail therapy*?

These considerations will all play into the type of franchise that will bring you satisfaction and joy and will help guide you to a business that you can successfully implement with conviction and passion.

Know Yourself

Choose something that feeds your soul.

One of the businesses I owned was successful in terms of providing the freedom, time, and money I desired. I eventually sold the business. I had a lot of people scratch their heads and ask me *why*, when it provided the freedom, time and money I desired.

The quick answer was that it did not feed my soul.

When I needed to put time into the business, my heart would sink, and I would get agitated. This went on for several years until I realized the pattern. This endeavor had very little positive feedback from clients (due to the nature of the business). Around this time, I had heard someone wise say that it is important to spend time on things that gave one energy, not sucked it from them. I decided to sell the business and pursue other opportunities that I would be excited to get out of bed every morning to build and run, and I have found myself exponentially happier.

Moral of the story - choose a business that feeds your soul, that makes your heart sing and that provides the passion and excitement to own and operate.

To ensure that:

- **Turn Your Search Inward**
  To successfully tackle the first strategy it's critical that you look in the mirror before anything else. Spend time getting to know yourself. What are your strengths? What are your weaknesses? What are your passions? I can't overemphasize the need for passion in whatever endeavor you pursue. Franchise ownership does not forgive inertia. Passion and the energy you bring to your business will power your business in ways that no amount of marketing or vision can accomplish. Passion is contagious and this characteristic will fuel your staff, your marketing, your creativity and the invaluable ways your customers will relate to your presence in their communities. Have a passion for your business- for example, don't open a gym if you don't personally embrace the benefits that a healthy lifestyle can accomplish. You can't fake passion and ultimately your business will fail if you don't walk the talk.

- **Recognize your Weaknesses with Humility**
  To this end don't get in over your head--hire and surround yourself with people who pick up the slack on tasks and have the skills

that you don't possess. Not a numbers person? Hire a competent budget and accounting person you trust.

No marketing background? While franchise ownership comes with the backing of corporate assistance and a marketing framework, go above and beyond and hire someone who understands and has experience with this critical need. Building a strong team that fills each segment of your business needs will alleviate your stress level, create more free time and deliver peace of mind that your business can work like a well-oiled machine.

Marketing

If your franchise is the hub of the wheel, marketing is the intricate structure of spokes to keep your vision together and provides the strength to your business success.

Marketing achieves successful communication of the personality of your business and your brand and needs to be consistent throughout all arms of the marketing funnel. From advertising, public relations, promotions, affinity relationships and social media your message needs to be clear and consistent to help customers identify with your brand and its positioning in the communities it serves.

Most corporate franchisors provide marketing tools and strategies for franchisees so you're not reinventing the wheel, but it will be up to you to determine your marketing budget and implementation.

The good news is, is you don't have to tackle this critical component of the business without a net--you'll have some level of directive and creative backing from your franchisor. Marketing, in all its nuances, is the sexy part of the business and can be the creative outlet to the dryness often associated with running a business. It's forgiving to the extent that if it's not working it can be changed up and improved, but it's imperative to keep it going. Spend considerable energy on this arm if you want to grow your business. It's one of the best strategy tools on your investment of money and time.

Seek First To Understand

In all aspects of implementing your business plan the first step is to seek first to understand. Because we so often listen autobiographically it's human nature to respond in one of four ways:

- **Evaluating** (you judge and then either agree or disagree);
- **Probing** (you ask questions from your own frame of reference);
- **Advising** (you give counsel, advice and solutions to problems);and
- **Interpreting** (you analyze others' motives and behaviors based on your own experiences).

In this way we can only project that which we have experienced and which we can personally relate to. Therefore, it's critical in business to step outside of our own frame of reference and be able to be open minded enough to step into someone else's story to truly understand the issue at hand. This takes a degree of humility and patience. This concept is understandably used in methods of conflict resolution-seek first to see the other's perspective.

Components include active listening as opposed to passive listening, which entails simply staying silent long enough to let the other finish speaking and merely reverting to projecting your own experience. But just as important is to seek to understand your own thoughts and beliefs, and to have enough humility to understand that what you think you know might not actually be true. Dismiss your own limiting beliefs and preconceived self-imposed boundaries. Employ this tactic when relating to your staff, your customers, your community at large and your colleagues.

Don't Go Down With The Ship

I learned this concept the hard way, without a net, but you don't have to.

With the first business I owned I made the rookie mistake of maxing out my credit cards and put myself into a dire financial situation before I realized that I was being too stubborn and inflexible in making changes and adapting.

The lesson here - recognize that even with the best vision, the strongest team and the best laid plans, sometimes the results will fall short of your expectations.

When this happens, it's critical to recognize it early on and take immediate steps to adjust the sails. Don't hope for the best and don't try to adjust the course without a clear path. Don't jump in without a net.

Flexibility, humility and courage are critical to affect positive results. Re-plan and pivot quickly at the first sign that something is not working. Remember the age-old rule of the definition of insanity - doing something over and over and hoping for different results. Assess, revise and implement a new strategy whether it's a marketing shortfall, determining your customers' needs, or addressing an internal conflict.

Change the course, change the ship, change the crew- it's not necessary to die on your sword.

These strategies are just the tip of the iceberg but the five basic platforms that I find the most valuable in initiating the change that you seek in your life. Become the change you want to see in the world and the world around you will follow. Know that your dream is possible! Freedom from conformity, time to live the life you truly desire, and financial success is possible to have all at once. I've done it. I've helped others do it and know it's possible. You can do it too- the key is to have your systems and processes duplicatable and scalable. The tools to successful franchise ownership have been developed to assist you in reeling in the life you desire and by employing these initial strategies you don't have to do it without a net!

About Matt Frentheway

Matt Frentheway has been inspired to have a positive impact on others' lives. From his start as a Financial Advisor to starting, owning, and selling several successful business ventures, Matt has the experience to assist others in achieving their personal and business goals. Today, Matt excels in pairing candidates with franchise opportunities around the country. He is excited about assisting his candidates in finding a franchise brand to buy and build their American dream.

Matt is a graduate of Arizona State University, having graduated cum laude in Agribusiness/Pre-Veterinary Sciences. He lives in Park City, Utah, and is the father of five sons, ages 12 to 22. When he is not assisting others in his consultant role, Matt enjoys wake surfing, skiing, snowboarding, and mountain biking with his family.

Connect with Matt today to find out how he can assist you in accomplishing your dream of owning your own business. He can be reached via email at *matt@learn2franchise.com* or *https://calendly.com/mattfrentheway/meet-matt* or via phone at +1 801-874-3009.

Contact Matt Frentheway

www.learn2franchise.com

https://twitter.com/mattfrentheway

https://www.linkedin.com/in/mattfrentheway/

https://www.instagram.com/learn2franchise/

https://www.facebook.com/learn2franchise

A Whistle Stop Tour Of Franchising

Darren Taylor

When I first started on my entrepreneurial journey I knew nothing about franchising. I was just looking for a business to acquire which could both help expand my wife's gardening work and create a job for myself.

A Google search however led me to discover franchising, and StumpBusters. After that I didn't consider any other opportunities, I simply knew a StumpBusters franchise was for me. In all honesty, in the beginning it wasn't the franchise side of things that interested me; I merely saw it as a means to an end. But the beginning is never the whole story.

Up until franchising, my experience was in technical sales, but I'd always had a desire to build and run my own business. As a young man, working within a commission structure was the closest I could get. Commission gave me a product to sell and income earned by my own performance, but I wanted more.

Franchising hit the sweet spot. It offered a kind of secure halfway house between the lack of challenge in selling for a company as an employee and the risky uncertainty of going it alone. In short, franchising was a revelation. It gave me the blueprint to create my own business based on a proven model and it also provided support. I knew how to sell well, but other things were less familiar. I discovered one of the benefits of franchising is that it helps you work on your weaknesses. Whatever you are unsure of be it sales, operations or something else, there is advice available as you start.

So is franchising a dead cert? Not quite. However, it is the best way to begin a business as you have the back-up and support of both a system and a franchisor. On top of this, statistics show that in franchising versus going it alone, banks are usually far more willing to lend to a franchise.

Occasionally still a franchise will fail. In my experience, such failure comes when an individual themselves fails to put enough effort in. I myself worked hard and got the rewards.

There are great opportunities for growth within the franchising model. Naturally, some of this will be organic, but more importantly once an initial territory is near capacity, there is always the next one to add. One way I found particularly effective for this growth was to acquire neighbouring territories from franchisees looking to exit. By this method, I ended up with three extra areas in addition to my first. I found that they could often be acquired for a good price and given I was already familiar with the franchise model, I could hit the ground running without unforeseen problems.

As my business grew, I still had the full support of the franchisor. They were there to help me with advice on employment and administration as well as purchasing larger, more productive machinery. I discovered too, that utilising the franchise's buying power was a great way to get the best price on that machinery.

Most franchisors will pro-actively help with growth because it is mutually beneficial. Franchisors want good quality, ambitious franchisees as they bring good rewards and very few problems.

After additional territories, the next step of my journey was quite a leap. It is a fact that I have always been very ambitious. This meant that one day I approached the StumpBusters franchisor to ask about acquiring the business itself. At the time they were not actively looking to sell, but they were interested enough to pursue my proposal. After three years of negotiation, the deal got over the line and I went from franchisee to franchisor.

Being a franchisor is a very different way of life. It is really rewarding when you see your model working and your franchisees becoming successful through your teaching and support. And when then, as a result, they start making good money and the management service fees begin rolling in – then you know why you are in franchising.

As with anything worth doing, it is not all plain sailing though. There can be some difficult days, such as when a person believes that franchising equals buying work. When that individual signs and their phone does not automatically ring, they soon start blaming you.

There is an on-going joke in the industry that when recruiting franchisees all you need is a cheque book and a pulse, but the pulse is not necessary. It's tongue-in-cheek, but the joke has a more serious side.

It is important to recruit ethically and without setting the bar too high.

Some of my best franchisees have turned out to be the ones who, in my head, only just made the grade when I signed them. Those who scrape in often have the fire in their belly needed to succeed.

Along with sound judgement comes the law. As a member of the British Franchise Association (BFA), I know there are many rules and regulations to be adhered to and with good reason. The BFA is well respected and I would always recommend new franchisors seek its help and advice. I would also encourage reaching membership status. This will give you credibility when recruiting and within your wider business. It can also assist you on those occasions when something goes wrong.

As a franchisor, there are multiple opportunities for further growth. Starting a new franchise from an existing business not currently in franchising may not be easy, but the rewards can be exponential. With your franchisees investing their money, happily you need not risk yours. However, it is important to always be careful and stay aware of the costs and other risks involved. To succeed you must be able to add value with your own experience and systems.

One powerful tool I have utilised is the R+D tax credit system. This government scheme encourages business owners to create new products. Having that piece of bespoke machinery or software will ultimately enhance your business and set you apart from the competition. It will also add value for any potential franchisee. In return for your work, the government will give you credit against your tax bill, or even cash should you make a loss. I have used R+D tax relief in one form or another with three of my franchises, saving tens of thousands in tax and creating excellent equipment at the same time. Altogether it put me ahead of the competition not only in the general market, but also in the recruitment of franchisees.

Beginning a master franchise operation is another way for your business to grow. Similar to starting your own franchise, this comes with all the challenges of recruitment. If your chosen brand is already known and successful in another country though, the task is slightly easier. In most cases a great deal of support is available, with original franchisors possessing a wealth of experience to be drawn upon. There should also be the extra value of existing bespoke software, IP manuals, contracts, health and safety processes, etc. available to you.

Master franchising is an easier option than creating your own franchise from a standard business. Often the best opportunities come from international franchises available within your current industry. This thinking and method worked for me when I bought a pest control franchise from the Netherlands.

Something else which I have on the whole found very successful has been acquiring brands. With experience in franchising, especially as a franchisor, there is always the opportunity of brand acquisition. Particularly brands with the same type of franchising as your own. For me, this has so far involved *man and van* type franchising.

Generally, this combines low investment, low overheads and low risk with fairly high returns. It is often easy to then grow your new brand into a bigger brand and even easier if the necessary ground work has already been done by its founder.

Once a franchise has reached 60-80% coverage in the UK, growth can become more challenging. Some franchisors stagnate at this stage, but there are three options open to ambitious entrepreneurs.

Franchising internationally is usually the first of these which comes to mind. Whilst it may be an obvious choice, I've personally found the cost and time required can make it very difficult. I signed my first master international franchise three years ago, but am still waiting to see any real return on my investment. Time will tell.

The second option is to sell out to a Private Equity firm. The third gives you the best of both worlds.

This option involves a model which has proved very successful for me, Agglomeration™. Created by my friend and business partner, Jeremy Harbour of Unity Group, the model provides a win-win scenario for franchisors.

As mentioned previously, brand acquisition is a great way to grow your franchising portfolio. By the time I had successfully bought and nurtured five key brands, I knew Taylor Made Franchising was ready for bigger and better things. With my original StumpBusters having been joined by PVC Vendo, Wilkins Chimney Sweep, Traas and Thomas cleaning franchise, I turned to the idea of public listing.

As a small to medium enterprise (SME), there was no chance of this on my own. However, public listing with Agglomeration™ made it both possible and profitable. The innovative model allows a group of SMEs from a specific industry to band together in one publicly listed holding company. Each entrepreneur in a group exchanges their private shares for public shares in the new holding company and joins the market. At this point in my journey, Franchising International PLC was born.

Public listing in this way provides the benefits of shared liquidity and big buying power.There is the opportunity to increase your company valuation and balance sheet position while ultimately still keeping control of your business, plus you will have a seat on the board of the plc with a one seat one vote basis so have influence of the direction of the plc. There are also the options to take some of your money off of the table and be paid in bonds.This means a 5% return on your sale value for five years plus your original money back at the end.

Joining other franchisors in a publicly listed holding company was a hugely positive step in my franchising journey and one I would sincerely recommend. If you are a franchisor looking for better rewards and aiming to grow your business, Franchising International PLC could also be for you, it is always expanding.Joining other franchisors in a publicly listed holding company was a hugely positive step in my franchising journey and one I would sincerely recommend. If you are a franchisor looking for better rewards and aiming to grow your business, Franchising International PLC could also be for you, it is always expanding.

So, is a public listing with all its rewards the next step on your journey too? Wherever you are at the moment, franchising is the best adventure.

About Darren Taylor

Darren Taylor is the Managing Director of Darren Taylor Holdings Limited, and CEO of Franchising International PLC that is currently based out of United Kingdom. He is an experienced Franchisor and Investor, currently dealing with mergers, acquisitions and turnarounds with various franchise networks.

Having graduated from Corfe Hills School, Darren has always dreamt of running and building his own business. As a young man, he started his career in technical sales – working as a Sales Representative from 2002 – 2007.

During his time as a Sales Representative, Darren came across the idea of franchising – a proven model that he knew he could dabble in, even in tough markets. He then realised the benefits of becoming a franchisor – thus giving him the revelation of creating his own business.

In 2006, he took on a franchise from Stumbusters in Dorset, after a year of great trading, he further took on West Hampshire, Bristol and Bath and finally Devon, with this success, he took the risk of approaching StumpBusters with the intention of acquiring the business and managed to get the deal – thus marking the start of his new career in 2013 as the owner of StumpBusters UK LTD.

Darren established Darren Taylor Holdings Limited in 2013 and has grown it into the company that it is today, with the acquisitions of Wilkins Chimney Sweep, Vendo commercial vehicle cleaning Traas Pest Control group and

Thomas Cleaning franchise. Having been recognised by the Best Franchise Awards for great service to Franchisees, Darren continues in 2020 the growth of his companies by founding Franchising International PLC and adopting the AgglomerationTM Model.

Darren is actively look to acquire invest or merge in all aspects of the franchising industry please see contact information below.

Contact Darren Taylor

http://linkedin.com/in/darren-taylor-b2b07132

darren@taylormadefranchising.co.uk

@taylormadefranchising

The #1 Factor To Success In A Franchise Business

Kim Daly

If you are exploring franchising or even if you are a franchisee already, you have probably heard that the #1 factor to success in a franchise business is following the system. While following the system is very important, there is something even more important to achieving success. This something is controlled by you and why only you can predict if you will be successful.

Before I tell you the #1 factor to success, I want to debunk the myth that it is the franchisor's responsibility to make a franchisee successful by sharing an analogy from my personal training days.

I want you to imagine that you and three friends join a gym on New Year's Day. All four of you have goals to lose weight and get in shape. Your goals vary, but you are all committed to achieving them. Instead of fumbling around the gym with no plan because you are smart enough to realize that absolutely does not work, you hire a trainer and decide to all train together in a small group.

So, you are in the same environment with the same trainer and working the same plan.

Fast forward a few weeks, do all of you start to see changes in your body at the same time? Maybe but maybe not. Does one of you drop a lot of weight really fast? Possibly. Does one of you gain weight? Possibly. Does one of you quit after missing a few workouts? Probably.

So, if you are all in the same environment with the same trainer and working the same plan, why don't you all achieve your goals at the same time?

Individual results vary because of genetics, focus, intensity, consistency, attitude and beliefs not to mention what happens in the 23 hours you are not in the gym. If results vary, does that mean the gym is not the place to get in shape and lose weight? Of course not! The gym is the place to achieve your fitness and weight loss goals. If all of you do not achieve your goals is it the trainer's fault? The trainer owns some responsibility in creating an effective workout, but the trainer cannot change your body. You are the only one who can change your body.

So, let's connect the dots between the gym analogy and success in franchise ownership.

In a franchise business all of the franchisees are in the same environment because territories and locations are demographically similar. Franchisees have the same training and the same plan like the four of you did by hiring the same trainer.

So why don't all franchisees achieve their goals at the same time? Because just as you and your friends had genetic variances that made your bodies respond differently to the same workout, there will be market variances that cannot be accounted for until a franchisee starts working the market.

Why do some franchisees fail while others go on to live the life of their dreams? Because franchisees quit, and because just like it was never the trainer's responsibility to make your body change, it is not the franchisor's responsibility to make you a successful business owner. The franchisor can perfect the system, the training, marketing and technology, but ultimately, those are just tools to aid you.

You are the owner of your success.

Your focus, consistency, determination, perseverance, attitude and even the size of your goals will determine how successful you are.

So, what is the #1 factor to success in a franchise business?

YOU!

Over the last two decades, I have been helping people realize their dreams of franchise ownership as a franchise consultant. I get to know my candidates and match opportunities to their background, interests, skills, finances and life goals. I guide their investigation helping them to know what to be focused on, who to be talking to and even what questions they should be asking.

A proper franchise investigation takes about one to two months, and by then, I can have my candidates competent in their due diligence so they can be confident in their yes!

Sometimes new candidates will ask me what my success rates are to which I reply that I do not own any success rates. I can expertly guide their due diligence, but what they do, how they show up: mentally, physically and financially after they say yes is 100% on them. Other times, candidates will ask me if I am going to tell them if they are not a good fit to own a franchise to which I reply no way.

Over the years, I have helped people who I thought would be rock stars who have barely succeeded, and I have worked with folks who I was not sure should be saying yes who have gone on to build multi-million dollar companies. Just like the personal trainer cannot predict who will achieve their fitness goals, I, too, cannot predict who will achieve their business goals.

A few years ago, I worked with a candidate named Rick who I really had reservation about working with. Rick was in career transition coming from a manufacturing background, and he was lifeless on the phone. He admitted he was an introvert, and business ownership would challenge him in new ways, but he was excited for those challenges.

Rick had always wanted to own a business. He was tired of the politics in corporate America and the lack of job security. Now that he had lost his job, he was committed to never going back.

As I got to know Rick, I felt a little better about helping him make this change in his life, but to be honest, I still hoped he would figure out this was not the right thing for him. He just did not have the outgoing personality that I thought a successful business owner had to have. I did not want to add insult to injury and put Rick in a position where on top of losing his job, he would lose his nest egg too. But, because the owner is the #1 factor to success in a franchise business, Rick defied all of my odds!

This man now runs a multi-million dollar company in the home services space. I partnered him with an incredibly strong franchisor who has world class systems, and Rick committed to those systems with his strong desire to never have to go back to corporate America. It has been nearly ten years, and I would say Rick is never going back to corporate America! He rose to the challenges of business ownership, redefined himself, followed the systems, used the tools, stayed focus on what he wanted despite the ups and downs of owning a business and just kept pushing forward. I could not have predicted Rick would be the success he is today, but he made his dreams come true! Rick is the #1 factor to his success.

Another great story with a surprise ending was when I met Mark who was a retired military officer, so right away, I knew Mark could follow a process, and he had great leadership skills. After retiring from the military, Mark had a corporate sales background, so I also knew he had communication skills. On paper, this candidate was a franchisor's dream!

One of the companies I found for Mark was a more established franchise in his area, so his zip code was already owned by another franchisee, but nearby there was a nice open territory with his name on it. To this day, I still remember Mark's first comment about the open territory. He said, "People in that city don't spend money like people where I live."

This would become my first experience in seeing how what people believe, they make true!

As with Rick, the franchise I presented Mark was an industry leading company with rock solid systems and operations. They were and still are a world class organization. As Mark explored all the companies I presented to him, he kept coming back to this particular franchisor, but he also kept stumbling over the territory and wishing he could own his back yard. As the franchisor got Mark out in the field interacting with the other local franchisees, Mark got more excited about joining this *family*, and ultimately, he decided to go for it!

Eighteen months later, the franchisor called and asked me if I would help them resell Mark's territory. Of course, I was shocked and disappointed not only that Mark failed, but that he never reached out to me for help. I knew his demise was not because of the systems or the territory. I knew it was because of what he *believed* to be true about that territory.

Tyler, the second candidate I found for Mark's territory, happened to live in that territory. He was also in career transition, but arguably was not as strong of a candidate on paper as Mark was. But, Tyler did not have any *head trash* or preconceived notions about the territory being second rate. He was ecstatic to have a business in his hometown and to no longer have to commute into work.

Tyler went on to become rookie of the year doing nearly one million dollars in revenue his first year in the same territory that Mark believed was not a viable territory.

What was the difference between Mark and Tyler?

The difference that made all the difference was what they believed. In business, and in life, we get what we believe. What we believe determines what we make true.

So, what is the #1 factor to success in a franchise business?

YOU! Your attitude, beliefs, focus, consistency, determination, perseverance and the size of your goals determines your success.

The franchisor can provide world class systems and tools, but it is up to you to use those systems and tools to build the business and life of your dreams!

About Kim Daly

Kim Daly is one of America's top franchise consultants who has helped thousands of people explore franchise opportunities. For nearly two decades, she has traveled the country as a keynote speaker and business break out leader and has hosted her own live events educating, motivating and inspiring Americans to the dream of small business ownership through the proven systems of a franchise.

Prior to becoming a franchise consultant, she ran her own health and fitness based consulting firm and worked with Dr. Denis Waitley, Denise Austin, eDiets.com, Gold's Gym and many other national health and wellness brands.

She launched the first health and fitness marketplace at USATODAY.com called BeHealthyNow. She was a personal trainer in college and a Miss America preliminary contestant. She graduated Summa Cum Laude with a degree in Nutritional Biochemistry and a minor in sports nutrition. Kim has been a business owner for over 20 years. She has the wisdom that comes from experience combines that with her knowledge of the franchise industry and passionate personality to inspire people to achieve their dream of business ownership.

In all her pursuits, she desires to be a role model and influence others to live their best life!

Connect with Kim Daly

www.TheDalyCoach.com

www.linkedin.com/in/dalykim

www.facebook.com/createwealththrufranchising

www.youtube.com/KimDalyFranchiseConsultant

Phone: 1.800.897.4937

Don't Be Distracted By The Shiny Stuff: Franchising And The True Route To Success!

Paul Mitchell

Wherever you look and whoever you consult with, I can assure you that if you do some research into franchising a business and in particular what makes a franchise successful you will more than likely find the following requirements listed:

1. The Right Business Model
2. Scale
3. Scope
4. Location
5. Market Saturation

So the bottom line according to those who apparently know best is that a successful franchise network begins with the right business model and proceeds with the amassing of the right scale and scope in the right locations, until they reach optimum market saturation.A bit of a mouthful!

What they are actually saying is a business looking to franchise needs to have an interesting brand that catches the eye of a potential franchisee, the business has been trading long enough to prove its worth, there is ample scope to make money and expand the business, it is in a good location and the market hasn't already been saturated with competitors.

Ok I get that, and it makes sense as a starting point, but what about the Franchisor himself – who is of course a crucial element of the business, without the Franchisor there would be no business to franchise after all.

So, I would certainly add to the list the following:

- Motivation
- Dedication
- Drive

To be highly successful a franchisor must be totally dedicated towards their brand, have a strong drive and motivation for success. A franchisors devotion towards the franchise on offer will deliver a positive brand experience to customers.

What I have found over the forty years that I have been a franchisor and the thirty years that I have been a franchise consultant, is that a franchisor is only as good as his business and if he detracts from his business by being heavily involved in the franchise process itself there is every chance he will let go of the reins and the business that is supposed to be the beacon of success will suffer and perhaps even fail.

Taking the foot off the brake could be catastrophic for a successful business and the business should always carry on as before without the distraction of producing a franchise network. A distracted business owner could mean that the business to be franchised could quite easily fail due to lack of leadership and therefore is no longer suitable to be franchised.

A Franchisor has to be good at what he does and that is continuing to run his business on a day to day business. After all if the core business gets into trouble there is nothing to franchise! and all of the hard work will have been for nothing.

My advice to budding franchise entrepreneurs is that they must spend 95% of their time running the business and only 5% of their time building the franchise.

That's not as easy as it sounds however as we all like a bit of excitement in our lives and that desire to grow through franchising can be fatally distracting.

Franchising can be the most rewarding when it is done right and doing it right means using the expertise that is out there.

It goes without saying in my opinion being a Franchise Consultant myself that the Franchising process should always be undertaken by a reputable Franchise Consultant who has a successful track record.

However, I see too often an often obsessive fascination with planning the systems and writing the documentation (what I call *The Shiny Stuff*) but what use is the world's best operations manual if no franchisees have been recruited?

Documentation is important of course and I am not trying to advise against it. There is a definitive documentation process and a Franchisor needs to start with a Prospectus to market the franchise on offer and a disclosure document (either a Franchise Disclosure Document (FDD) or a Franchise Information Memorandum (FIM) dependent on where the franchisor is based in the world to ensure that prospective franchisees know exactly what they are buying into.

Beyond this, there has to be a document that instructs a new franchisee on the Franchise business methods, systems and day to day running of the franchise and this is the Operations Manual. Normally a huge document of around 300 pages and more.

But at the end of the day if interested parties are not converted into franchisees none of this paperwork has any value and there is no-one to use the shiny new Operations Manual.

Putting in place either an internal recruitment resource or outsourcing to a consultant who focuses their efforts beyond the *shiny stuff* is an essential first step in rolling out a franchise.

The business owner as I have said previously should continue to focus on running the business not the franchise.

Working principally in the UK, I see very few if any franchise consultants focusing on franchisee recruitment because the things that frustrate the franchisor and also makes the process laborious and expensive also affects the consultant– who will certainly prepare the necessary documentation and perhaps advise on where best to promote the franchise but when it comes to finding that nugget of gold in that ever increasing pile of coal; Franchisors are almost certainly left to deal with the enquiries and search out that elusive franchisee themselves.

The internet has created an incredibly easy to access marketplace for franchisees, there are dozens of franchise aggregation websites offering an often-bewildering range of options and choices to prospective franchisees.

A bad day at work, an unsettled night and the would-be franchisee is surfing the net searching for their new life. One click of the mouse and they are in a Franchisors inbox; if anything it is actually probably a little too easy for them to contact the Franchisor?

However, hundreds of enquiries lead to an enormous drain on the Franchisors time and energy. It's not just a click of a button for the Franchisor once those enquiries start to roll in.

Speaking to all of the people who have enquired and then meeting with those identified as potential franchisees is an enormous task and if they also don't have a total understanding of timescales and how the process works this can be extremely time consuming and take the franchisor away from the core business.

I don't like to blow my own trumpet but in my role as a franchise consultant my team and I make franchisee recruitment the core of what we do and our priority is to ensure that the franchisor does not need to be involved in the recruitment process until prospective franchisees have been vetted to an inch of their lives.

It takes in excess of 100 enquiries to recruit one franchisee and in many cases it can be significantly higher still. I have seen brands which have a very high level of prospect engagement require over 200 enquiries to recruit one franchisee.

In essence, the more a prospective franchisee likes the sound of the brand, the more difficult it will become.

For example, I have a brand that brokers the sale of high-end cars through their franchise network. Who out there doesn't fancy the idea of dealing with Ferraris and Bentleys throughout their working day? The result however for the franchisor is an ever more complex mix of cold, warm and tepid prospects. It takes time to wade through an ever increasing inbox in order that a new franchisee can be engaged

Beyond this, our increasingly digital world has created an environment where having enquired about the franchise opportunity the prospect doesn't actually want to fully discuss it. Email, WhatsApp and other messaging technologies are great for engaging with friends and family but in order to have a meaningful business conversation, two parties need to actually talk to one another.

Franchise Consultants come in many shapes and sizes but what a franchisor should be really looking for is a consultant that can not only develop the franchise for marketing purposes but can also recruit franchisees and that recruitment is actually a core part of their work.

As an alternative to an external resource, the franchisor

can of course manage the recruitment process internally. However, an experienced Franchise Development Manager will cost the franchisor in excess of £60,000 per annum in salary plus bonus and benefits.

Alongside this, there is the need to invest in solid systems and marketing. Franchise prospects do not have a 9 to 5 timeline and they will generally enquire outside of business hours, they will also enquire about multiple franchises. The business will need a robust lead management system that will auto-engage by email and ideally SMS with prospects instantly at the time of enquiry; leaving it until the following day or worse until Monday morning for weekend enquiries just isn't a viable strategy.

Thereafter, there has to be the assumption that the prospective franchisee may almost certainly not be at that watershed point immediately. The decision-making process for many applicants may be weeks or even months. There is therefore a need to build into the system some weekly and monthly *trickle marketing* to keep the message fresh in their minds.

My final advice on this subject is that if business owner looking to Franchise would prefer to do all of this internally, they should without doubt employ a full-time franchise development manager or alternatively engage a recruitment focused consultant who will have the team and experience to offer a complete package.

Either way a business owner shouldn't be tempted to attempt the whole process personally and at all times should not be distracted by those who want to concentrate only on the *shiny stuff.*

About Paul Mitchell

Paul has been a franchisor for 40 years and a franchise consultant for 30 of those years, as founder and Managing Director of Accentia Franchise Consultants Ltd, he works with clients across a wide range of sectors creating and developing franchise systems.

Bilingual English/Spanish, has experience as both franchisor and consultant across the globe and has created and developed franchise networks in Europe, USA, South Africa and Australia.

'Accentia' is the UK's leading franchise consultancy, with 12 regional offices nationally and an office in Dubai serving the Middle East and South Asia, the company has a strong emphasis on franchise network development and recruits over 1,000 franchisees annually for clients.

Contact Paul Mitchell

Website: *https://www.accentia-franchise.co.uk*

About Paul: *https://www.accentia-franchise.co.uk/meet-the-team.html*

LinkedIn: *https://www.linkedin.com/in/paulmitchellfranchiseconsultant*

The Hidden Secret Behind The Success Of "Would You Like Fries With That?"

Aveline Clarke

"Would you like fries with that?"

We all know how powerful those words are and how they helped create a permanent transformation in the behemoth franchise empire of McDonalds. When you walk into a McDonalds store anywhere in the world, you expect to able to order the same food with the same promptness and service standards, whether you are in country Arizona USA, suburban Adelaide in Australia, or an inner-city store in Bangkok or Paris.

When you place an order, you will always hear, *"Would you like fries with that?"* or *"Would you like a drink with that?"* – or whatever you did not order. We all know that's part of the operational blueprint of McDonalds every time, consistently, anywhere in the world.

Yet despite the repetitive offering of this upsell, it's not always very successful.

You may remember occasions when you ordered something at McDonalds, and heard the dreaded words, *"Would you like fries with that?"* How it grated on you like the sound of fingernails running down a blackboard, and you quickly replied, *"No thanks"* to speed up the transaction.

Yet it has remained a core aspect of McDonalds training and operational procedures, and they put much effort into ensuring that each staff member says it consistently each time.

There are even harsh penalties if they miss saying it, even once!

This verbal upsell is a process built into their training and operations because it supports the sales of the business. It is also measurable, tangible, and is a compulsory part of the training of all customer-facing serving staff members, and each new franchise must adopt it.

There's a secret to the success of this verbal upsell of, *"Would you like fries with that?"* which is not obvious at all. It is overlooked because, when we think about constructing a successful franchise, we focus on the blueprint of consistent processes, consistent systems, and creating a business model that a franchisee can replicate.

The secret to success with the upsell, *"Would you like fries with that?"* is surprisingly not about the systems and processes. It's not about staff training or how many times a person has said it or whether they have adopted it as a habit.

It's about WHO the person is delivering it, WHO they are delivering it to, and what they BELIEVE as they are saying it.

Sounds easy right?

It's a bit more complicated than it sounds, which is why it's not as effective as it could be, when delivered by a teenager or someone who doesn't have the awareness and understanding of the depths of engagement possible within the human connection.

The engagement of our hearts and minds in the human connection is always the secret to developing a meaningful relationship, and therefore creating the optimum sales environment for an enhanced customer journey.

So, the secret to the success of this verbal upsell is a HUMAN one, based on WHO they are delivering it to, and being able to use emotional awareness to connect those elements to make the journey for the customer a memorable and engaging one. And when you figure out how to do this, the upsell becomes easy, effortless and enjoyable for both parties.

I'll give you a first-hand example.

It was one week before McHappy day in Australia. On this day McDonalds donates $1 from the sale of every Big Mac to a children's charity and attracts people to their stores in record numbers across the country. Sales are at their highest, and they need their store full of staff to cope with the constant, day-long stream of customers.

I was 16 years old, and I'd just heard the exciting news that I was rostered on Register One, for the McHappy Day lunch shift at my local store. Our store was highly competitive for sales volume and was aiming to hit a record sales target on McHappy Day. There was a lot of pressure on the staff to be at the top of their game, be ready to work hard and keep the high standards up during their shift. Register One was the busiest register in our store because it was the first one people came to as they walked in. So, it was an honour and a big responsibility for me.

I was both nervous and excited.

To add to the pressure, we worked alongside our assistant managers, who would constantly be looking for excellence in our work. And following all procedures including the dreaded verbal upsell, *"Would you like [insert the item they didn't order] with that?"* on every sale.

I'll admit I hated it.

The upsell was the worst part of my job, and I always tried to get away with not doing it if nobody could hear me. But on McHappy Day there was no way to get out of it; I was going to have to say it every single time. As I was on Register One, I would also be on show to everyone around me.

I was excited because I wanted to prove to my managers that I was one of the fastest and most efficient workers. I wanted to shine and share in the accolades of record sales on this special day for McDonalds. And that is precisely what happened; our store broke its own sales records.

A week later, when our Store Manager shared the overall results and handed out awards to the few staff members who had excelled and contributed to the enormous success of the day, I was proud to be one of those staff members.

I was not only proud of my achievements inside our store; I was also proud of myself because I had mastered the upsell, for real! I felt like I'd climbed a mountain and achieved something well beyond my limitations.

Here's what happened for me on McHappy Day.

When my shift started, the store was already full, with several people lined up behind each register. I started my fast and efficient serving, quickly falling into 'the zone' of operating at my best. We were so busy, I was running on auto-pilot, and wasn't even thinking about the words coming out of my mouth.

"Would you like fries with that?"

"Would you like a dessert with that?"

"Would you like some cookies with that?"

As my manager was always around, I had to do it every time, even though I detested doing it.

I knew that the average upsell sale was a metric they would look at after they finalised McHappy Day numbers. Something inside me wanted to try and get some upsells into my transactions, even though I hadn't been very successful at it before.

The first hour of my shift went by in a flash. I did the upsell on every customer, and delivered the line, without meaning, in a monotone voice. There was a *"no"* or *"no thanks"* answer every time. I felt flat, rejected and unhappy with that response.

Then something inside me shifted.

I needed a better response from my customers. So I looked into the eyes of the next customer and smiled, waiting for the recognition and response from him. And I changed the delivery of my questions from a rote line devoid of passion and care, to one that sounded more conversational and personal. I wanted to get a positive response from my customer, so I asked in a way that actually showed I cared.

His response surprised me; his eyes opened wide, and he smiled. I realised I had a connection with him and took the opportunity for the upsell. I was nervous but asked him if he wanted a dessert with his order and delivered it while smiling and maintaining eye contact with him.

He said, *"Yes"!*

My thoughts were a whirlwind, and my insides were doing cartwheels. It worked! It was amazing, and I wanted to keep doing this over and over again to prove to myself that I could do it.

Over the next few hours, I served over a hundred people, making a connection with every person as I offered them the upsell. Unaware at the time, I learned later that I had broken a store sales record for the highest number of upsells achieved in a lunchtime trading period.

What I didn't know then, was that I had just learnt the difference between following a process without human connection, and following a process with a human connection.

I learnt how to engage with a person in a sales transaction and make them feel good. I also learnt how good it made me feel, and that it created an alignment between us allowing a relationship to form.

I also learnt how human engagement and alignment with

people made the customer journey more effective and enabled the business results to be better.

I had no idea at the time how pivotal this was, or what it was I had learnt. I just knew that it was something special and that it certainly wasn't part of the training I received as a worker at McDonalds.

The human connection in your Customer Journey is the most crucial factor in its success. The degree to which you can create engagement and alignment with your customers will determine the potential success of your business.

This is the hidden secret in ensuring your replicable processes are successful as you build and grow your franchises.

And always remember that people are at the core of ALL businesses. Mastering the connection with them both as your staff, and customers, is your key to success.

About Aveline Clarke

Aveline Clarke is Australia's first Infusionsoft Certified Partner. She is the Co-Founder and Marketing Director of Success Wizards, a Digital Marketing Agency that helps Small and Medium Businesses to achieve excellence by innovating their customer journey.

Passionate about integrity, trust and acceptance for all people, Aveline has perfected a process of customer journey mapping and innovation that helps businesses and industries understand their gaps, create a solution, and realise the true profits in their customer journeys. Her vision is to return the integrity and trust to the journey for the customer, the business and industry.

She has vast experience from small to medium businesses right through to large corporate organisations in mapping, creating and building customer journeys using principles of human behaviour and clever marketing automation technology. These redefined journeys deliver profit-enhancing outcomes whilst returning integrity and trust to the business.

Contact Aveline Clarke

Website: https://www.successwizards.com.au

About Aveline: https://www.successwizards.com.au/meet-aveline

LinkedIn: https://www.linkedin.com/in/avelineclarke

The Making of a Frantrepreneur: Why The Franchise Community Needs Purpose-Driven Leaders Now More Than Ever

Brian Holmes

With COVID-19 taking its toll on many industries, I know one thing is certain: when economies turn down, entrepreneurs turn up.

As a franchise veteran who has sat in multiple roles on different sides of the table, I firmly believe in franchising as a path to business ownership and entrepreneurship. The Frantrepreneur, a hybrid of purpose-driven tenacity and respect for systemized networks, is needed now more than ever.

It is up to the Frantrepreneur to decide what kind of impact we want to make in the world: we can continue to participate in the system passively, or, we can forge a new path.

When purpose becomes our guide, the frantrepreneur is

able to tug at the golden thread of success more effectively than ever before.

Especially in times of crisis, we're all analyzing how we can take smart risks, how we can be transparent – but inspiring – with our employees and customers, how we can survive.

While there's no such thing as a crisis playbook, I believe in a fundamental truth that's held steadfast for me in my journey: In order to survive a crisis, you must find a way to double down on what you already are as a company. This can only happen when you have an ironclad sense of purpose as a leader.

I started my franchisee and entrepreneurial journey in 2006 as a 23-year-old who had very little money but big dreams. On a flight home for Christmas I read the book *Rich Dad, Poor Dad* and I knew I needed to make the leap. Along the journey I almost went broke multiple times, made lots of mistakes, and sometimes I wonder what kept me going. The truth is I just don't know how to quit.

Since then, I've been involved with five different brands and owned over 30 franchise locations over the years.

My experience and passion for franchising led me to start the Franchise Story Podcast where we interview top-performing franchisees and the founders behind the brands they invest in. I started the Franchise Story Podcast to serve the franchise community— I figured if one listener can be empowered to make a change from listening to a guest's story, it would be worth it.

As we near the 100th episode, I'll say this—

I've had a refreshingly honest conversation with the former

CEO of Dunkin' Donuts, where he gave honest advice about bridging the gap in the franchisor/franchisee relationship.

I've met with the CEO of Firehouse Subs who showed me that customers choose you based on your values.

I've also spoken with some of the biggest names in the multi-unit world about how they've been able to scale the way they did.

I've heard the rags-to-riches stories, the keep fighting stories, and the stories passed down from family legacies.

Through all the business advice, the one realization that we all affirmed is this: the best thing about franchising is being in business for yourself, not by yourself.

Franchising is all about self-ownership, entrepreneurship in its highest form. It's also about community. Franchising has become my life and my community— all of my closest friends are fellow franchisees. I've learned as much if not more from the people in my franchisee community than I have learned from my franchisor. Boiled down, the help that I've received from other franchisees has taken me from struggling to success.

Currently, I own businesses that develop and operate boutique fitness franchise locations in California and Texas with my amazing wife Adrian. Now a grizzled franchise veteran, my existing community is more tight-knit than ever. It's one of the things that makes franchising so unique: Franchisees aren't competing with each other, we're helping each other grow. Those who stay isolated very rarely succeed. More than in any other industry, there's a strong linkage between community involvement and business success.

My other franchise business grew naturally as a result of my passion for helping my community and a desire to own my own franchising story more fully.

Franchise Ramp was started by Franchisees for Franchisees. Our purpose is simple: to help other franchisees achieve their entrepreneurial dreams. My co-founder, Peter Hansen, and I are both multi-unit, high-performing franchisees. We were tired of working with digital marketing agencies who didn't seem to understand franchising or business in general. So, we took matters in our own hands and became Facebook Experts (which is not as easy as it sounds). We hired the best and brightest social media marketing experts in order to provide targeted marketing strategies that maximize success for consumer-oriented franchises.

Peter and I have seen the power of social media on our business first hand. It's how we opened cash-flow positive from Day 1, and how we stay at the top of the ecosystems we're a part of.

Franchise Ramp's mission is to drive results that matter to franchisees through tech-driven, scalable, and measurable digital marketing solutions. Our values can be summed up in three words— We Live Franchising. Our mission serves as a behavioral compass while our values act as the set of directions to get us there.

Our purpose is really what sets us apart from competitors though— to help franchisees attain financial freedom and realize their entrepreneurial dreams. It takes outward focus to a whole new level, not just emphasizing the importance of serving franchisees or understanding their needs, but the ability to put our employees in customers' shoes.

From Franchise Ramp's origin, our purpose was, and still is to this day, the heartbeat of the organization.

While we've already seen the impact and consumer response to the COVID-19 pandemic in different states, a rollercoaster of new rules has turned many reopening strategies on its head in ways that are hard to feel prepared for. As complicated as the times are, our job as digital marketers remains a crucial requirement for recovery: to reassure consumers about the future and give them some sense of confidence that the future is something that they should invest in.

Having a sense of purpose in challenging times is more important than ever.

In my mind, there are three possible barriers that can prevent businesses from productively engaging with others in times of crisis in a purpose-driven way:

1) not being able to help,

2) not knowing how to help, and,

3) not believing your help is important.

The process of articulating your purpose and finding the courage to live it is the single most important developmental task you can undertake as a leader. While an alarming number of franchisors and franchisees may not be able to grow, mature, and strengthen their brand as they expected, the Frantrepreneur is able to take purpose and turn it into real impact.

In my experience, the path to business success is never

made unsuccessful by circumstances, but by a lack of purpose and meaning. Especially in the franchising world, it's purpose-driven entrepreneurs who enable a more rapid recovery in hard times. We're able to operate with fortitude, grit, and determination. We're able to manage risks in hard times and good. We're able to see that our business flourishes, for the betterment of ourselves and our community.

About Brian Holmes

At 23-years-old and right after walking out of his job in the banking industry, Brian Holmes bought his first franchise.

He struggled to build a business the old school way for 10 years but grew his business to 19 locations and $3 million in revenue – breaking organization records. He purchased another franchise with the development rights for four locations in the fitness industry. After he discovered the power of social media to grow his brand, he launched three locations cash flow positive from day one. Brian is the CEO of Franchise Ramp, the premiere franchise digital marketing agency built for franchisees, by franchisees.

Contact Brian Holmes

franchiseramp.com

brian@franchiseramp.com

LinkedIn:https://www.linkedin.com/in/brian-holmes-0a448566

Facebook: https://www.facebook.com/profile.php?id=1948036

3 Key Systems Your Franchise Needs

Pieter K de Villiers

Clearly defined systems and processes are one of the keys to any successful business. When you are franchising your business, the importance of your systems and processes is magnified, as you scale and replicate your original business.

Think of it like a picture on a balloon. When the balloon is small, the picture looks just fine, but as you blow up the balloon, all the cracks in the ink or lines not quite meeting up starts to become visible. Go far enough and the picture starts to be unrecognisable.

The trick is to create the systems and processes now, as if your business is already scaled. Draw the picture as if the balloon is already blown up.

Where To Start?

Start with the way you think about your business.

In truth, your franchise needs only three key systems.

Yes, these systems will be made up of different components, and as your franchise grows and your network expands, you may need to update or replace some of the elements, but your business will still function inside these 3 key systems.

What are the 3 Key Systems I hear you ask. Good question, we'll get to that.

First, I want to share with you just three of the reasons for having clearly defined systems and processes in your franchise.

1. You'll be able to focus on growing your network

With no discernable systems or processes in place, every day is a first day for your business. Neither you, your staff nor your customers will be sure how the day is going to go, and how things will be done.

The real-world effect of this is more time spent fire-fighting, managing mistakes from your team and inbound customer service queries.

By creating clear systems and processes in your business, you are able to create a minimum level of service and an undercurrent of activities which are there all day, every day.

This means you only need to get involved when there is an anomaly, which will be another opportunity to improve your processes and systems.

2. Look at the horizon, not your feet

When everything in your business is manual and *on the hoof*, it is near impossible for you to do any planning or *big thinking*. All your time is taken up by dealing with *now*, and 'now' never ends. This means you are just treading water and trying to stay afloat, making no forward progress.

What clearly thought-out and developed systems and automation gives you is the ability to look up, focus on the future, and actually make progress getting there.

You'll be in a position to create a business that *works*. A business that works for you, and produces results, with much less demand on your actual input and time.

What do you do with this extra time? You plan for the future, because it won't be like today.

As Keith Cunningham states in his book, *The Road Less Stupid*: "You need to run the business that is generating income today, whilst at the same time building the business that will generate income in the future.

If you spend all day fire-fighting, this is impossible.

3. New team members become assets to your business

In most businesses, and most businesses are not successful, a new team member starting goes something like this:

John, meet Sally, she's been with us for a couple of years now.

Sally, John is just starting, can you show him the ropes right?

And that is it.

John's only insight into how things are done in your business is what Sally tells him or shows him.

John will have no real focus on what is expected of him, because he is spending his time trying to get to grips with a couple of different pieces of software. There is nothing to guide John on what he is meant to do when he shows up for work on a Monday morning, so he just focuses on the can that rattles the most.

Before you know it, it is Friday, and John has still not learnt all that much about how he is helping to grow and build the business. Leaving it to John to figure out, means it can take up to six months before he is a profitable member of the team.

With the right systems and processes in place, and some automation, John will know exactly what to focus on next, and be able to tell important from urgent.

Back To The 3 Key Systems

Every business you've ever come in contact with has the same three systems. Yes, there are smaller sub-systems and processes nested under each of these. However, focussing on the three key systems will allow you to remain focussed and make progress optimising your business sooner.

Lead Generation System

Your lead generation system has one job - allow people to raise their hand and declare their interest in your product or service. That's it.

- Digital Marketing
- Print Ads
- Branding
- Blogs
- Podcasts

All of these are ways to get your business in front of the right kinds of people, and when they are ready and in need, it should be very easy for them to raise their hand and indicate their interest.

Prospects can raise their hand through:

- Completing a form on your website
- Starting a conversation with a chat tool on your website
- Commenting on your business' social media pages
- Responding to an email
- Direct inbound phone call
- Returning a direct mail form

The key is that you need several options that make it as easy as possible for someone to get in touch in a way they are comfortable with.

Client Acquisition System

This system is a bit like a sausage machine or a factory - Take the raw materials (Leads) and process or convert them into fulfilled output (Clients).

The Client Acquisition System works from the moment someone has raised their hand up to the point where money or contracts change hands.

- Automated email follow-up
- Social media retargeting
- Direct mail
- Telesales
- Face to face meetings

All of these functions sit inside your Client Acquisition System, it is like the heart at the centre of your business. If it stops pumping, you'll have no sales. At the same time, if you stop supplying it with leads, it will grind to a halt.

Client Fulfilment System

This is simply how you do what you do.

The distinction though is that the aim is not to just fulfil the service or order. Your aim is to have every client or customer feel fulfilled by the overall experience of doing business with you.

Here using the right tools for your business becomes critical. Up to this point, you've not had to focus on the specifics of your business. (Running Facebook ads for all businesses use pretty much the same tools and processes)

You want to ensure you are not running your business with software created by someone who knows nothing about your business. Don't shape your business to fit around a single tool or piece of software. Just because you have a hammer, doesn't mean everything is a nail.

But my business is so much more complex!

As you will know, business is more complex than a three step process. There are several systems and processes nested inside each of these three key systems.

Think of it this way though:

A security and safety system is a single integrated system. It would be made up of:

- Burglar Alarm System
- CCTV System
- Fire Detection System
- Flood Detection System

Each of those are made up of components, but together they function as a single security and safety system.

Looking at your business through the lens of the three key systems, you'll avoid getting stuck in all the micro details before you've even started.

How do you optimise and automate these three systems?

First, identify where the lines and responsibilities are within your business, mapped onto these three key systems.

Keep in mind that right now, some of your team might work across more than one of these systems. Be clear though, any of the tasks and functions they perform, will only ever sit in one of these three systems.

Work on the systems in reverse. It sounds counterintuitive at first, but you need to start by optimising and automating your Client Fulfilment System. This helps to ensure that when you strike gold with your Lead Generation System, your business can cope, and the wheels don't come off.

Next you move to the Client Acquisition System followed by the Lead Generation System.

Recap

Three key systems, with three specific functions:

- Lead Generation System - Allow people to raise their hand
- Client Acquisition System - Turn leads into clients and customers
- Customer Fulfilment System - Get the work done. Deliver to your clients.

Always keep in mind, you'll be building two sets of these key systems:

One set for the business you are franchising, to be used in each of your franchise locations.

The second set will be for running the franchise business itself, finding, selling to and supporting your franchisees.

Focus on these, and you'll be well on your way to building a successful business you can scale and franchise.

About Pieter K de Villiers

Pieter K de Villiers is a Co-Founder of Macanta Software Limited and a Small Business Systems and Automation Expert, working with Business Owners and Franchisors to Design, Systemise and Automate their businesses, in order to free them up to focus on the growth of the business, instead of the day-to-day.

In his role as Chief Product Officer, Pieter leads the design and development of Macanta, as well as working with Partners and Clients on system design and implementation.

Pieter is married to Sophie, an oncology consultant, with two daughters, Amélie and Olivia.

Pieter is a massive music fan and a bit of an audiophile (Tubes Rule!!). He enjoys watching Rugby (Union - South Africa/Wales/Harlequins), Cricket (preferably at Lords), Snooker (Come on Ronnie!), Formula 1(Mercedes) and Tennis (Rafael Nadal).

Contact Pieter K de Villiers

Website: *www.macantacrm.com*

LinkedIn: *www.macantacrm.com/pieterli*

The Global Vision Mindset

Haroon Danis

On the 23rd of March 2020, the UK went into lockdown. The COVID-19 pandemic meant that all of our revenue streams suddenly stopped. We have a chain of five skin clinics providing treatments to clients via face to face appointments. So suddenly we found that our growing chain of clinics had no revenue streams. It was a time of worry.

We did know one thing, that over the last three years our clinic has been able to replicate its model in five different cities across the UK, not just the larger cities but also, the smaller cities. We have been ready to get them all fully booked with clients, and they always made high revenue. With the lockdown, we had to find new revenue streams, so we started by changing the website to an eCommerce site. This allowed us to post our products to our registered clients.

We had a great response, and it confirmed that the brand we built is resilient to even the shutdown of our main revenue streams and that our client retention is strong.

This gave us the realisation of the value of our brand, and we then had a look back at how the industry was affected during the last recession and economic crisis - the great recession of 2008.

And what we found was that our industry had grown through this crisis.

The current crisis is a health-related crisis since the pandemic significantly caused the recession. So, clients can not get their treatments, but we soon learned that when we offered the eCommerce store, there is still plenty of clients who wanted to buy products from our site. The clients have maintained a relationship with the clinic, and by supporting this relationship, the clients only turned to SkinHQ for their skincare needs.

Looking back, the only thing that held us back from opening more clinics was it took a certain amount of time to build the teams, to employ the staff. Had there have someone invested in the new locations, then it would have been much easier to get more sites opened at a faster pace.

One thing that we had planned before the lockdown but never entirely completed was to franchise our business.

In such uncertain times, it would have seemed risky to franchise the clinic, so to do so we had to do a great deal of research. From knowing that we are included in the industry that grows during the recession and further to the response of our clients. With website sales virtual consultations increasing. We started to realise that in a downturn, there would be so many other businesses that would not have the same positive outlook. And the beauty industry was one of the few industries that seem to be coming out strong, even during uncertain times. We went back and kept this positive mindset. By looking at the analytics, we felt it was the right time to launch the SkinHQ franchise opportunity. From there, we went to see our solicitors get contracts complete, work out all the models. So, with the support of the solicitors, we got our franchise agreements, modelling completed and launched the SkinHQ franchise.

We felt the timing was perfect as we were aware that for people in other types of businesses, other industries and sectors, times were looking quite bleak. Maybe they would be interested in getting into our industry since we have a proven track record where we could demonstrate our continued growth, location by location over the three years of our business. We have this mindset and this confidence that we gained from our success our records speak for themselves.

To get the interest in our franchise opportunity, we created an advertisement all about *freedom*.

We had the view that people would be feeling locked down financially also so the feeling of financial freedom would be one that resonated with the potential franchisee partners. We used a video we made all about freedom and repurposed it to promote financial freedom, not showing anything to do with the clinics, just someone enjoying their life and being free holidaying around the beautiful scenery of Bali.

We added some text over it saying, *"Want to become part of a brand with a global ambition"* and just some small insights that we are launching a franchise scheme. It raised lots of interest. Following that, we then re-marketed to the viewers with a video that is a lot more about our actual clinic and the franchise opportunity. This technique worked perfectly, and we received 1,200 applications within two weeks on our website from people that wanted to apply to get a franchise. We were completely blown away. The inquiries came from the UK, and all over the world, the response was terrific.

The type of people that inquired are people from the engineering world, medical world, entrepreneurs from other sectors that have been negatively affected by this pandemic and realise they have all their investments in one industry. And when their industry gets affected, they may consider investing in another industry, which has a slightly more positive outlook during these times.

Franchising is an excellent way for investors to spread their investments across different markets, and this became clear from speaking with the potential franchisee partners.

So really from there, we started signing franchises, and we also discussed our master franchises internationally for several different territories.

When we launched the franchise, we had a target of opening maybe one or two franchises a year. With such a tremendous response, we quite easily surpassed that within the first month. So, it tells you that it is all about having a positive mindset and attitude, learning from the available data. Understanding that if you have a business that has a tried and tested formula and has shown steady success in numerous locations, then there are investors out there that will be willing to invest in opening a franchise of your business.

Now, ultimately it is one of the fastest ways to open more locations and grow your brand globally.

With more locations, we have many benefits, not only the monetary value of the income that we will receive but also the buying power for all the products, all the equipment and machinery. There is a marketing levy percentage of sales from each location which we can use together to invest in much bigger marketing campaigns than any individual clinic could afford by itself.

For me, one of the best benefits is that we have more people financially invested in the brand.

A great example of this is one of the first franchisee partners we took; Robert is a psychotherapist and clinical hypnotherapist. At SkinHQ, we have long been exploring the theory that there is a link between skin health and mental health. Saying this, we have no mental health specialists within our clinic. Still, from our experience and analysis from the feedback that we get from our clients, they feel much better with their mental health once they visit our clinic and they may have some skin problems that could cause issues like anxiety and stress for them.

On the other hand, if they also have suffered from mental health problems, this can cause an outbreak of skin issues. We are not specialists in this area; all we know is that we try our best to keep our clients happy. If our clients are satisfied, then their skin health can also improve. Bringing in a Robert with his expertise adds to our service. Robert also agreed with our theories and will support us in exploring them further so we can better understand all the causes that affect our clients' skin health to provide a more comprehensive service ultimately.

Franchising allows you to invite partners who have

specialities in other fields that are outside your own. This creates a great space for regular and constant improvement for the way we deliver services and the business of skincare throughout all of our locations.

I think the best thing that we have learned is during this time of change; we have the positive mindset to keep pushing forward, to look at the numbers, look at the statistics, and look at what history has taught us. We were able to keep the positive mindset to keep pushing forward that led us even to try to launch the franchise during the lockdown in the first place. And the response that we received just showed that this is just the best way to proceed if you have a business that can demonstrate its success.

If you know, you have got a business that is working, and you have been able to replicate that company in multiple locations successfully then there will most definitely be investors out there who are looking to invest in your franchises.

It is sometimes difficult to look at your business in a way that a potential investor would look at it, but the way we look at the situation and the way the investors have responded about why they found the opportunity so attractive. We had a business where someone could invest a certain amount, and from the statistics of previous financial results, we can show them when they will receive the return of their investment, and when they should expect to start making a profit.

Also, another huge attraction is that the franchise will have the support of our centralised call centre and marketing team. We have always been able to get our clinics busy from the launch, and a franchise partner will not need to be concentrating on how to generate the clients as this will all be taken care of centrally. Also, this gives us the franchisor an insight of quality control as well and being able to make sure the revenue streams flow as they should. As a franchisee partner, they do not have to make the mistakes that we did when we first started as we have learnt from those mistakes and can guide them accordingly.

We have a proven successful formula which is the main attraction.

We always had a global vision for SkinHQ, which was to improve skin health while creating good secure jobs all around the world. Now we are much closer and much more successful at achieving that vision through franchising. Had it not been for that vision, we may not have gotten so far because every time we create a job in SkinHQ, we are creating more opportunity for someone to have their skin health improved. And the more skin health we improve, the more jobs we create.

Franchising has helped us accelerate our vision moving forward. I hope you can also benefit from our story.

About Haroon Danis

Haroon Danis is one of Great Britain's most promising young entrepreneurs. 2020 could have been a year of negative consequences for business owners however Haroon's dynamic and adaptive approach to business has meant 2020 is looking likely to be one of SkinHQ's biggest to date. Haroon is inspiring both personally and professionally and has a vision to make world changes far beyond his current reach.

SkinHQ believes in not only making people look their best but also empowering people to feel their best. It is Haroon's vision to create as many good stable and secure jobs across the UK and internationally. Haroon is a finalist in numerous awards in 2020 which includes the Lloyds bank National business awards in the New Entrepreneur category, The Starling Bank Great British Entrepreneur Awards in the Fashion and Beauty category and he has taken SkinHQ to the finals of the Growing business awards in the Young Company of the Year category.

Contact Haroon Danis

Website: http://www.haroondanis.com/

LinkedIn: https://www.linkedin.com/in/haroondanis

Instagram: https://www.instagram.com/haroondanis

Facebook: https://www.facebook.com/HaroonDanis

Let's Get Virtual: How To Sell Franchises Online

Tommy Balaam

Why It's A Great Time To Sell Franchises

2020 has certainly had its challenges, but with every bump in the road there's always an opportunity for something great. Many people are facing hardships with work, money and worries about the future, praying for a lifeline that could offer some hope. If you can frame the offer of your franchise so that it touches on people's pain points and offers solutions to their problems, you're probably in with a good chance of a successful sale. The prospect of starting up a new business in these uncertain times is incredibly daunting. However, with many people being furloughed or made redundant, the opportunity to buy into an already successful business might be just the thing that offers them a way out of their current situation.

Since the pandemic, global interactions have drastically changed. Flying across the world to attend meetings and conferences has morphed into joining a Zoom meeting and getting to grips with the mute/unmute button. The world has changed so it's important that you change with it, and fast. The ease of joining a conference online has allowed many to forgo the stress and money spent on travelling and has greatly increased the accessibility of important meetings. This is especially useful when trying to sell a franchise because those you wish to sell to, by the very nature of franchising, probably won't be in your area. It's time to capitalise on this.

Who Am I?

My name is Tommy Balaam and I'm the proud owner of Captain Fantastic, named the 'UK's best children's entertainment company' by the reviewing site FreeIndex. We have over 1000 5 star reviews online and have worked for clients such as Hugh Grant, Nickelodeon and the BBC. I set up the company 10 years ago after graduating with a BA in Acting from the East 15 drama school; during this time we've won many awards, including a 'What's on for Kids' award and a 'Junior Magazine' award. Our Facebook following has grown from 3k to 65k during lockdown, and we've been interviewed by Sky News and BBC news for our online parties and free Facebook lives; we were also featured in The Telegraph for our ability to adapt our parties so that they worked virtually. Alongside Captain Fantastic, my business partner and I set up Ambitious Arts. This company is intended to help performers use their skills in order to create successful businesses that can financially support their creative careers.

I think we were similar to many people in thinking that '2020 would be our year', then March happened and poked a sharp hole in our party balloon of optimism. However, by quickly adapting our approach and business model to fit this Brave New World, we were able to capitalise on the possibilities that the virtual world had to offer; selling franchises online being one of them.

How

The skills needed to sell franchises in person are no different to the skills needed to sell franchises online, all that differs is the approach. After successfully selling four franchises during lockdown, I have been able to create a step-by-step guide that will help others to do the same.

1. Pre-Registration For Your Online Webinar

One of the companies I own, alongside Captain Fantastic, is Ambitious Arts. In our book *Pain in the Arts* we've released the Product Pathway we use to coach performers with their businesses: attract, bewitch, captivate, delight, engage, fulfil. Following these steps allows you, as the business owner, to take your customers on a journey that will enable them not only to buy from you, but also to fall in love with your company and what you do.

The first stage - attract - is what you're aiming for when getting people to pre-register for your online webinar. You want something that's eye catching, exciting and will grab people's attention. Finding a good image and carefully selecting what accompanying text to use when putting this advert out, is key. You'll want to keep the text minimal, so as not to overwhelm your audience in a way that would put them off reading all of it. Advertising through social media, using paid ads to boost outreach, has been our most successful method. When boosting your advertisements it's important to know your target audience. This will ensure that your money is spent in a way that reaches those you desire to reach (creating an avatar of your ideal target audience could be useful). It's also important to make sure you have a Landing Page as this will allow you to convert people's interest into sign-ups. A Landing Page will enable you to collect relevant data and contact information for those interested in buying a franchise.

2. The Webinar

There is lots of funky, high tech software available that you could use to run your webinar. However, these are usually costly and not entirely necessary. My business partner and I have found Facebook Lives to be a highly effective medium when running webinars and Q&As. People can log on with ease, it gets rid of any scary idea of commitment/formality, and it allows people watching to engage through the comment section. If you're looking to give your webinar that extra glean of professionalism, I'd highly recommend a streaming site called Streamyard that can be linked to Facebook and Youtube. The features on offer, such as: banners, tickers, backgrounds, the ability to bring comments up on the screen and play videos before/during/after your talk, will really give your stream that extra *je ne sais quoi.*

The ideal length of time for this webinar is around

45minutes; when you reach the end you can open up the virtual floor to any questions from your adoring fans (he says optimistically). Returning to the Product Pathway set out in section 1, this stage of the journey would fall under the 'bewitch' and 'captivate' phase. Ideally, you'd want to use this time to sell the dream and opportunities that buying into your company will afford your potential buyers. It's important that you stay positive, fun and upbeat during this webinar. This isn't the time to go through logistics, this is the time to inspire, excite and communicate your selling points. Make sure you highlight their potential salaries, the economic freedom it will offer, the business training they'll get for free and the satisfaction of this extremely rewarding job. Before the final Q&A let them know where they can sign up to your Discovery Day (which will detail the logistics, the 'how') and collect their contact information so you can be sure they receive the details for the next event. To summarise: during your webinar you should be selling the opportunity as one that's shiny and fun; allow them to dream themselves into your company.

3. Virtual Pre-Drinks

Virtual Pre-drinks isn't an official 'step' in the same way that the webinar and the Discovery Day are. I'd recommend linking this event to your Discovery Day and holding it the night before, as a relaxed way for everyone to get to know each other. Whilst seemingly the most informal part of the process, this actually tends to be the most revealing and informative gathering, from your position. To go on a slight digression - I was recently watching an interview with one of the ladies who cast the kids in the movie ET. After finding who they believed to be their 'perfect Elliott', the casting directors invited all the children to play Dungeons and Dragons together and quickly realised that their 'perfect Elliott' was domineering and unliked by the other child actors. They therefore decided to restart the casting process and eventually decided upon the Elliott we all know and love - Henry Thomas.

One should never underestimate the importance of getting to know the people you'll be working with in settings that allow you to see who they truly are. Playing games or socialising with a couple of drinks often gives you much greater insight to a person's true character. It's a chance for you to properly assess their suitability for the job, especially when you're looking for someone to take on the responsibility of representing and running your company. The Pre-Drinks doesn't have to last long, maybe an hour or so, and in this time you can get to know each other, go through any questions they might have about the Discovery Day, and show them how to log on to the meeting.

4. The Discovery Day

This is your main event, your chance to 'engage' and 'fulfil' your potential franchisees and really pitch your company and the opportunity it will offer. This will most likely take place via Zoom and should last about 3 hours. It's up to you how you choose to structure your time, taking into consideration exactly what needs to be communicated and how. I usually reserve the first 10-15 minutes for a bit of friendly chatter, which has the added benefit of allowing for latecomers without having to repeat any information once they arrive.

One of the benefits of holding this Discovery Day online, particularly on Zoom, is that you can record the session and send it out to everyone later that evening so they can go over any details they may have missed. Providing you keep yourself spotlighted and you send them the 'Speaker View' version, the video will only show you and nobody else.

During these three hours I tend to go through what each franchisee will be receiving after buying into the company. This will include things like: equipment, support, CRM capabilities, business coaching, finances, etc.

Since my company is entertainment oriented, I also opt to perform set bits from a few of our shows. This helps demonstrate value and skill, while also allowing people to see the type of thing they'll need to be able to do should they end up buying a franchise.

During your webinar, you probably only would have had time to go through the *what* and the *why*; therefore, the Discovery Day is an opportunity to go through the *how*. This often ends up taking quite a bit longer, but it is vital if you want your potential business partners to fully understand what they're buying into.

Taking them through a typical week as a franchisee would definitely be of interest to them and would give you a chance to set out your expectations. Going in with a timeline that notes where you'd expect them to be after the first month, first three months, first six months and first year would also be of use.

However, no matter how much you sell and push your franchise, the people buying into your company are going to want to know that what you've said is truly achievable.

What better way to demonstrate the very real potential of your opportunity than by having a couple of your top franchisees talk at the event. People might be wowed and excited by the figures you offer, but if you want them to connect emotionally, then your best chance is giving them someone to relate to. Encourage your franchisees to be honest, especially when it comes to talking about the fears and worries they had when signing up. If they're able to talk openly about their own struggles and how they managed to overcome them with your guidance, this step will enable everyone attending to make the connection between the dream you're offering and the reality of it working for them.

5. The Follow Up

At the end of your virtual Discovery Day you'll need to ensure that you follow up with those who attended, or else all your hard work would have been for nothing. It's vital that you don't leave the ball in their court; people have busy lives, and even if they are interested, the likelihood of them getting back to you without any prompting isn't high.

For this reason, it's vital that you take control and book in follow-up phone calls with everyone who attended. Arrange the calls to take place the following week - this will give them enough time to digest the information, but not too much time that they forget about you and move on.

It's important to note that, at this stage, you won't be trying to sell to everyone. Although the emphasis thus far has been on you selling your franchise, by this point you'll probably have a good idea about who you'd actually like to work with. It might be that somebody is keen on buying into the company, but having got to know them through the Pre-Drinks and Discovery Day you've spotted some attributes you don't feel would be a good fit for your company. You'll want to funnel your potential buyers at this point and spend your time selling to the people you believe are the right fit.

Acknowledge your own power and know that, ultimately, you have been auditioning them - not the other way around.

Good luck and happy franchising!

About Tommy Balaam

Tommy Balaam is the founder of Captain Fantastic, voted the UK's no. 1 children's entertainment company. Following the company's success, Tommy created a Captain Fantastic book series. Both the parties and the books are dedicated to captivating young audiences with bold characters, plenty of laughter, an emphasis on children's wellbeing and, above all, exciting stories. The brand is now growing nationwide and expanding to include a YouTube series, music albums and online games.

Tommy trained as an actor, graduating in 2009 from the East 15 acting school. As well as acting, Tommy has a love of music and performs regularly with his band, Dirty Mitts.

Alongside Captain Fantastic, Tommy and his business partner created Ambitious Arts. This company is intended to help performers use their skills in order to create successful businesses that can financially support their creative careers.

Contact Tommy Balaam

Tommy@captain-fantastic.co.uk

Twitter: *www.twitter.com/cfparties*

Facebook: *www.facebook.com/captainfantastickids*

LinkedIn: *www.linkedin.com/company/captainfantastic*

Website: *www.captain-fantastic.co.uk*

5 Fundamental Components Of The Successful Evolution Of A Franchise Network

Robert James

(Editor: At the time of publication Robert James is writing about the long range implications of the 2020 pandemic on franchising.)

The successful evolution of a business idea into a thriving franchise network is a huge challenge!

The vast majority of people who attempt to franchise their business will fail. You would think that with all the resources available globally franchise success would have become easier.

Actually, the opposite is true.

In 2020, we have more small business owners than at any time in history, but we have declining franchisee numbers. The patent reflects that many potential franchisees aren't seeing the valve in paying franchise fees to franchisors.

In today's world, small business owners don't necessarily need a franchisor to teach them how to run a successful small business anymore. There is an abundance of online experienced experts to teach, support, mentor or educate small business owners in any business.

On top of this trend, the pandemic (2020) changed the rules of business dramatically and constantly. As I write, many franchise systems will collapse; others will survive and thrive. But this is true of any time.

So, why do some Franchisors systems succeed, while most fail?

There are Franchisors who are beating the treads. They are growing successful franchise networks that deliver for their customers, franchisees and themselves despite challenging circumstances..

Ongoing Evolution Of Their Business

Franchising is survival of the fittest. Evolve or die, especially in 2020 in a world experiencing unprecedented changes. The constant evolution of the franchise business model on all levels is vital.

It takes an extraordinary collaboration of these five fundamental components that create the lifeblood to the Successful Evolution of a Franchise Network.

- A small business system is commercially proven.
- Science based logical thinking.
- Emotionally intelligent Leadership

- Creative Solution environment
- Ethical Pragmatism in the Leadership

Let me explain.

1. The Foundation Small Business System Is Commercially Proven

Firstly, the business system has to be profitable for the franchisees. A valid proven commercial venture built on proven small business systems that have a track record of success in the marketplace. All business systems require formal documentation in a format that is franchisee user friendly.

Clearly, the relationship is commercially based. The relationship has to deliver a win/win for all involved. Both, the franchisees and the franchisor have to commercially flourish. The numbers have to be achievable for everyone involved in the business.

There are franchisors selling franchises that are not commercially viable. They make their money form the initial franchisee fees and rely on the "Churning" of failed franchisees. The franchise opportunity looks like a "good idea" and that may be the case, but a good idea has a lot of evolution to go through to be great business opportunity.

Proven commercial success therefore vital; failing base business equals failing franchise network.

2. Science Based Logical Thinking

Franchise evolution requires a great deal of science in the leadership thinking and the approach to developing robust systems that deliver efficiencies, and sustainable profits. The definition of Science is the systematic knowledge of the physical or material world gained through observation and experimentation.

The mantra is: Test, measure, improve and repeat.

A successful Franchisor embraces their inner mad scientist and systematically tests and measures their businesses constantly to find ways to improve the systems.

There is one scientific law that is essential for all franchisors to accept as actuality is *The Law of Probability.*

The law of probability tells us about the probability of specific events occurring.

The law of large numbers states that the more trials you have in an experiment, then the closer you get to an accurate probability.

Reducing the risk of failure of the franchisee is a key responsibility of every franchisor. A great franchise system is consistently using The Laws of Probability to give their franchisees the most likely chance of success.

Franchisors shouldn't ever expect their franchisees to hope a new idea or an existing franchise proposition to work. The franchisees aren't there to be used as an experiment in untested systems.

All systems within the network should designed to give

the most likely successful outcomes - already - before you onboard franchisees.

3. Emotionally Intelligent Leadership

The commerce and science sounds very logical but of course we require people to run the business to service more people.

Ironically, with all the logical foundations based to commerce and science, it's the emotional energy of the motivated people that drives the business on every level: the Franchisor or master franchisors; the franchisees; and the staff.

A Franchise network is a very unique business environment. The relationship is NOT the same as a typical Boss & Employee arrangement and this can be confusing to both parties.

Many franchisees are first-time small business owners coming out of employment in regular jobs. They make the big move to become their own boss but head towards a franchise because they believe the franchise is a safer option presumably with proof of concept.

Many Franchisors treat Franchisees like employees who can't just walk out the door and get another job. Standover management approach over a coaching mentoring relationship.

It requires a high level of emotional intelligence to understand the emotional requirements of a large group of independent family-run, business owners who are that various stages of their own business evolution.

To make this even tougher there is a constantly altering emotional energy. The constant fluctuating variables of the group creates an "Group Attitude" that is continuously fluid.

Why is a Franchise Network's "Group Energy" so volatile? Because most franchisees have everything riding on the success or failure of their business creating a high level of intense emotional energy.

- **New franchisees are terrified of failure:** That is good and bad. Good: if it motivates them to learn quickly or/and try harder. Bad: If worry and panic creates fear that makes them implode. This can fluctuate between positive and negative on the hour or day depending that the individual.
- **Failing franchisees:** Businesses failing are a cancer that will eventually engulf the whole network. Failing franchisees actively contaminate other franchisees, regardless of what is making them fail. The business model, the Franchisor or the Master Franchisor or the Franchisee or COVID19 pandemic.
- **Personal stresses:** I have helped franchisees navigate nearly every human emotion and personal tragedy know to man. From failing health, divorce to death of a family member. These tragedies are happening to people every day and they affect their attitude to their business.
- **Successful franchisees**: Once they reach a level of confidence franchisees becomes a positive influence on the group attitude. A network that has a strong long-term group of successful positive franchisees will have a less volatile *Group Attitude* as a whole. If a high percentage of long-term successful franchisees are leaving the network to pursue their own independent business this will undermine confidence in the group.

The goal is franchisee retention strategies.

- **Growth:** A rapidly growing network will have foreseeable growing pains. In a growing franchise, introducing new franchisees will be constantly shift the group dynamics.
- **A changing business environment:** The 2020 Pandemic is the obvious example: we live in a rapidly changing world and franchisees don't like change. Most people join a franchise network for stability, consistency and security. Shifting circumstances can undermine those values. In times like this, franchisees expect more of the franchisor. When *Change* is a necessity for evolution, change management is vital.
- **Emotional Intelligence:** The *Emotional Intelligent* component in the successful Evolution of a Franchise Network is the key area that the vast majority of franchisors fail in. It takes strong emotionally intelligent leadership to understand and lead any volatile business environment let alone a network of franchisees.

4. Creative Solution Focused Culture

There is a special creative skill that can turn any idea into a successful reality. It takes imagination to visualise the concept, belief in the final result, a creative mind to build the solutions and a determination to see it to the end.

Top performing franchise network embrace an ongoing creative solution focused environment that is proactively working on "making things better".

When COVID19 pandemic hit Australia/world many franchise networks were turned upside down. Overnight franchisee's businesses were thrown into chaos.

Franchisors who already had a culture focused on creative solutions went into *solution* over drive.

McDonalds Restaurants, for an example, on top of their usual menu, they very quickly started selling bread, milk, eggs and hand sanitiser at their drive through windows. Then a marketing campaign to inform their customers of their new services.

A creative solution using what resources that were already available to their franchisees that was available over night but was a reflection of decades of Creative Solution Focused Culture.

5. Ethical Pragmatism In The Leadership

The evolution of a successful franchise network is a long, tough and sometimes winding road. There will be many predictable and unpredictable challenges. There is nothing that can completely prepare any Franchisor or Franchisee for every future obstacle or goal.

Things will happen, good and bad.

Those things will have to be dealt ethically and with a high level of pragmatism.

Leaders who vigorously deal with all components in a practical effective ethical manner lead toward the survival of the whole network.

Pragmatism is the adhesive that holds all the 5 Fundamental Components together to lead to the evolution of a long-term successful franchise network.

Evolution Of A Franchise Network

In 2020; And Beyond

2020 has turned our world upside down, and we are heading into a new world where the only thing for certain is we are facing a world of uncertainty. The focus is on compliance and safety, of course, but also innovating within that framework.

Many Will Fail

The Franchise Sector is facing colossal challenges over the next 2 to 5 years. Many franchise networks will not be able to evolve their business systems quickly enough to survive the next 2 years.

Many outdated or ineffective business models or uncommercial franchise opportunities will vanish over the next two years.

Others Will Evolve And Thrive

We will see other Franchise systems that will evolve and thrive through those uncertain year. They will be built on these 5 Fundamental Components.

There will be Established Franchisors who pragmatically supply emotional and financial support for their franchisees to help them get their businesses in the other side.

They will have creatively found business solutions that they are both financial and logically based. Invested plenty of emotional energy to keep the *Group Attitude* in a positive healthy state.

They certainly will face challenges for themselves and their franchisees, but they will evolve ethical pragmatic solutions that gets the best results under the circumstances.

There will be *New Age Franchise Systems* that are born from finding opportunities in the current unstable business environment. The business systems will be designed to flourish in unstable and emergency business environments and beyond.

They will thrive using current technology to outperform traditional style franchise businesses in their sectors. Their franchise opportunities' will meet the new market attitudes and buying habits in more effective, profitable and smarter business model.

Out Of The Ashes Of 2020
The Franchise Phoenix Will Rise

By mid 2020, many economies around the world are heading into recession. Businesses are failing. Jobs are being lost. Unemployment levels will reach new unseen highs. Families are truly hurting. Things are going to get worst before they get better.

Franchising can be part of the solution on the other side. The Franchise Sector historically thrives in recessions and high unemployment. The by-product of an uncertain employment market is that there will be more people deciding to take control of their future and start their own business.

The Franchise networks that evolve a high value, low risk franchise opportunity that exceeds the expectations of potential small family business owners have a bright future.

But there is no shortcut to the Successful Evolution of a Franchise Network.

It's remains a huge challenge, but it can also supply great rewards to everyone in the network, if is built on fundamental components.

About Robert James

Robert James has a proven record in business. He is passionate about helping business owners grow their business while maintaining as strong connection to their family. He has been a leader and mentor in the franchising sector of over 25 years.

At the age of 21 he first entered the business world as a professional horse trainer and breaker. By 27 years of age he commenced his franchise network James Home Services, which grow to a 400-strong franchise system and turned over $20 million in home services annually.

Robert is the multiple bestselling author of: *Balance: How to make your family and business life work together* and *The Ultimate Guide to an Extraordinary Services Business.*

Robert has mentored Franchisors and Master Franchisors or more than 25 years.The current"James Family" business is Balance Enterprises that helps Franchisors and independent business owners to use grow their businesses through systemisation and mentoring positive leadership skills. The focus is always making family businesses work for the family.

Contact Robert James

Web: https://balance.enterprises

LinkedIn: https://www.linkedin.com/in/robert-james-1b44b6ab

Twitter: https://twitter.com/jamesmaster99

Facebook: https://www.facebook.com/robertjames99

Ultimate-Guide-Extraordinary-Service-Business: https://amzn.to/3l9eYmb

Balance: https://amzn.to/3aNKK3g

Get This Wrong And Nothing Else Matters

Andrew Priestley

You can do everything right, but if you get this wrong, I can predict your franchise is at risk of stagnating or stalling.

As a general rule most businesses do not ask their customers how they are going … and most customers won't usually complain to the service provider if there's something they are unhappy with. But they will tell everyone else!

With that in mind:

1. If you ask your clients to identify the key frustrations they have with you, your business or your industry… they will usually tell you
2. You then have a pretty good to-do list of things to fix in your business … that if you actually fix them … your clients will actually appreciate; and

3. That usually results in more repeat business, referrals and new business.

Don't take my word for this.

A couple of years back I was engaged by an established plumbing company to help explore the potential for creating a plumbing franchise. After several strategy days with the management team we decided to focus on developing a compelling customer experience that would differentiate the proposed franchise from other plumbers.

Starting with a customer survey.

Plumbing is plumbing but as our surveys showed *how* that solution is delivered and the subsequent customer experience is a deciding factor if you focus on the key metrics of repeat business; positive reviews; and referrals.

We interviewed 317 customers about home services per se. We collated their anecdotes, and listened to their key concerns, frustrations and complaints with:

1. Any recent specific experience with a service provider; and
2. The *home services industry* in general – carpet cleaners, electricians, tradesmen, bricklayers, carpenters, plumbers, dog washers, pest controllers, etc; and
3. Any anecdotes about our specific client's service offering.

We then converted that feedback into a report with recommendations and then shared the feedback at a number of in-house workshops.

Guess what?

There were a lot of complaints, but nothing any business can't fix easily that will improve your delivery and get you more business and referrals.

Your customers are a gold mine of valuable information about you and your business ... but you have to *ask* them. And you have to listen to the feedback. Regularly asking all your customers for feedback - at or around the time of service delivery - will result in valuable feedback ... if you *act* on it.

As a rule of thumb, you can get good general information from eight people (a focus group), better detail from 32, more useful information from 120 and invaluable 'shades of grey' from 300-1,200 customers.

Fortunately, you can do a lot yourself for free or inexpensively like emailing questionnaires or in our case, have someone phone or visit a customer for about a ten-minute chat.

With permission, we recorded the interviews, had them transcribed and analysed the feedback.

The participants were residents drawn from postcodes within the territory of focus. And they were interviewed about their experience.

We asked about:

- the service being provided
- a description of the tradesperson (i.e. male or female)
- perceived level of expertise, competence

- what they experienced
- an informal 1-10 Net Promoter Score rating i.e., 1-5 being Dissatisfied, 6-7 being OK; and 8-10 being Very Satisfied; and
- whether they would recommend, refer or buy again from that provider; and why.

We tabulated the issues on an Excel spreadsheet. Basically, every time a certain complaint was mentioned, it scored a point. (This is a very basic overview of the procedure.)

We then rank-ordered the service complaints. Number 1 scored the *most* mentions and so on.

Seven Key Complaint Categories

We found some key themes.

- Communication/Relational
- Competence
- Confidence
- Manner/Professionalism
- Consideration
- Honesty
- Safety/Security

Two key factors: were competence and manner.

Competence

The tradesperson was either perceived as skilled and competent and inspired trust and confidence; or unskilled, inept and incompetent and fostered a sense of concern or distrust.

Manner

This describes how the customer experienced the service provider i.e., professional, considerate, polite and easy to work with; or unprofessional, inconsiderate, rude and a concern to work with.

The general recommendation is to be good at what you do; and to be consistently professional in all your dealings with customers. Seems obvious right?

What Else Did We Find Out That Is Important To You?

We identified four stages linked to the total service experience. They are:

- canvassing/lead generation
- quoting for business
- service fulfilment
- post service delivery/follow up

You need to be mindful of how you handle each of those

important stages. What you do or don't do in these four stages impacts on your ability to win work and importantly, repeat business and referrals ... irrespective of the competitiveness of the quote, expertise or availability.

Mainly Men: Why Are We Not Surprised?

In most cases the interviewee levelled their angst against male service providers i.e., didn't listen, rude, late, BO, creepy. There were instances where the complaint was about a female service provider, i.e., pushy, flirty, patronising but these were few. Key suggestion: monitor your men.

Some Key Findings

We identified 39 key complaints but the following out number everything else combined. They are guaranteed to get customers hot under the collar.

#1. Didn't turn up on time, as agreed, or at all!

Tradespeople are notorious for being late or not even showing up. Everyone values their time. A LOT of customers arrange to take time off from work to be at home to suit the availability of the tradesperson. Then they show up late - with no apology - or; not at all.

As a rule, show up on time, as agreed.

Tradespeople typically spread themselves thin time-wise; and geographically. In most cases, jobs take longer than estimated; and travelling to jobs takes longer than expected.

There seems to be an across the board problem with time management - even if there's a system for time management. We are still staggered at how many tradespeople don't run a diary; and tradespeople who book jobs at random geographic locations – which almost guarantees they'll be late for the next appointment.

Apart from being a profit killer, the customer is guaranteed to be annoyed, deem you unreliable and not repurchase. Incidentally, this was also the number one reason customers switched suppliers!

Let's pretend you start a franchise called *Mow-On-Time* that has a policy of arriving on time as agreed … *or the service is free*. This means you better sort out the logistics of booking and travelling to jobs, zero excuses. It might mean you only book jobs within a specific area that allows you to arrive on-time as agreed.

If you are always late and not punctual for appointments expect customers to switch. If this is you, re-read this point.

Our clients discovered that 80% of their business comes from within a 12 mile radius of base. Postcode analysis showed they started to lose money on customers located more than 12 miles away. This alone was a good reason to franchise their offering.

#2. They didn't want to do what we agreed

Time and time again we heard that tradespeople didn't do the job properly as requested or as agreed.

For example, one person we interviewed had hired seven mowing firms – ALL franchises – all promising to remove the garden waste (i.e., lawn clippings, pruned trees, leaves etc). To a man, everyone of them had overlooked the removal of garden waste!

We found a variation on this theme for plumbing franchises: no mess Charlies routinely leave a mess.

#3 It wasn't right but I couldn't get them to come back (quickly or at all)

This complaint surfaced again and again. There are a several excuses:

- **You are genuinely busy.** You've got lots of work scheduled and you don't have the resources to do timely reworks. I recently spoke to a plumber who said he works from 5am to 9pm most days on new business, let alone reworks.
- **You can't afford to go back.** I discovered that to win the job you probably had to price the job very competitively. So there is no margin for a rework hence your reluctance to go back and fix any issues. This usually shows up as you don't or won't go back. Basically, dishonest. If you read ZMOT you will learn the power of reviews.
- **You are no longer in business.** Did you know most fencing contractors who offer lifetime guarantees on their work are longer operating as a business three years later?

But ... the customer doesn't care. They want it fixed!

#4. I felt unsafe

Customers are very security conscious now. This issue is a clear stand out.

"This big grubby, hairy guy turns up to my front door wearing a sweaty t-shirt, a leather hat and work boots … with NO ID tag, NO business card, NO brochure, NO vehicle signage, NO uniform. He could have been anyone! We didn't let him in."

Customers definitely feel more nervous especially if they can't identify you because you don't carry any identification. Identification can be a simple as a business card, a brochure or a plastic name badge, a name embroidered on a uniform, right through to a personalised photo identification badge and operator number. The Mormons have this sorted why can't you?

Your customers WANT to FEEL secure. They definitely want to feel SAFE in their own home. They don't want to feel intimidated. Franchise operators who get this one right win repeat business simply because their customers feel safe regardless of their competence.

#5. He didn't listen

Customers had a LOT to say about poor listening (and poor communication in general). *I told him what I wanted ... but then he did the exact opposite! He built an amazing shed ... next door.*

The world is becoming more relational so right here is an argument for ongoing communication skills training.

There were 39 big complaints that we identified across seven categories. Every one of these invalidates your marketing and the money you spent on getting customers.

But you need to know that ALL of the issues are easy to fix; should be included in ongoing training; and should part of a standard performance review of all team members - especially if you are building a turnkey franchise,

In the 1950s a guy called Igor Ansof proved that the easiest person to sell to is an *existing customer.* Existing customers spend more, more often. And they are your marketing department. They refer.

In addition, now they leave online reviews that last forever. Think: Trust Pilot, Trip Advisor or Amazon. You must download Google's stunning *Zero Moments of Truth (ZMOT)* report about how people search and buy online, now.

No matter how good your franchise value proposition is, getting the customer experience wrong - and allowing your people to get it wrong - will cost you a fortune. It will negate any money you spent getting a customer. And it will shred dollars off the *lifetime value* of your typical customer.

Getting just little things right, and making that a feature of your customer experience, will build you a loyal customer base. Get it right *consistently* and rolling that out across your franchise network, and driving accountability on a robust customer experience, is a license to print money.

Whatever conditions and circumstances.

Just ask your customer.

About Andrew Priestley

Andrew Priestley is an award winning business coach who specialises in leadership development. He is rated in the Top 100 Entrepreneur Mentors UK; lectures at CASS London School of Business on entrepreneurial studies and is a bestselling author of five business books.

Andrew is also the Chairman of Clear Sky Children's Charity UK which provides play therapy for vulnerable children aged 4-12 who have experienced or witnessed a trauma; he is a strategic advisor to The Mahler Foundation that promotes the legacy of Gustav Mahler globally and serves on several Boards.

He loves playing music and cooking.

Contact Andrew Priestley

www.andrewpriestley.com

https://www.linkedin.com/in/andrewpriestley

Would You Like To Contribute To Future Editions Of Franchising Freedom?

Our first outing of *Franchising Freedom!* has been a #1 international best-ranked, bestseller.

If you would like to get involved in the next release, then please get in touch. We'd love you to share your current best franchising thinking, experience and strategies that will inspire, educate and add value to franchising entrepreneurs globally.

If you would like the Writer's Guide, then please email:

coachbiz@hotmail.com

Lightning Source UK Ltd.
Milton Keynes UK
UKHW040931290920
370684UK00009B/45

9 781912 774708